10/25 24-99

A German General on the Eastern Front

A German General on the Eastern Front

The Letters and Diaries of Gotthard Heinrici, 1941–1942

Johannes Hürter

Translated by
Christine Brocks

Pen & Sword
MILITARY

First published in Great Britain in 2014 by
PEN & SWORD MILITARY
an imprint of
Pen & Sword Books Ltd
47 Church Street
Barnsley
South Yorkshire
S70 2AS

ISBN 978-1-78159-396-7

A CIP catalogue record for this book is available from the British Library.

Typeset by Concept, Huddersfield, West Yorkshire, HD4 5JL.
Printed and bound in England by CPI Group (UK) Ltd, Croydon CR0 4YY.

Pen & Sword Books Ltd incorporates the imprints of Pen & Sword Archaeology, Atlas, Aviation, Battleground, Discovery, Family History, History, Maritime, Military, Naval, Politics, Railways, Select, Social History, Transport, True Crime, and Claymore Press, Frontline Books, Leo Cooper, Praetorian Press, Remember When, Seaforth Publishing and Wharncliffe.

For a complete list of Pen & Sword titles please contact
PEN & SWORD BOOKS LIMITED
47 Church Street, Barnsley, South Yorkshire, S70 2AS, England
E-mail: enquiries@pen-and-sword.co.uk
Website: www.pen-and-sword.co.uk

Contents

List of Plates

A burning village on the Eastern Front. 'It is like the Thirty Years War, the same habits and customs' (19 November 1941).

Soviet soldiers in Moscow. 'Equipped with phenomenal winter gear, he penetrated the wide gaps in our front' (22 December 1941).

Winter on the Eastern Front. 'In early February we had blizzards for three days' (6 February 1942).

Thaw in spring. 'Now it has been thawing for a couple of days' (20 April 1942).

Preface to the English Edition

I still remember the day fifteen years ago when I discovered the private papers of the Wehrmacht General Gotthard Heinrici in the Militärarchiv of the German Bundesarchiv in Freiburg. The tremendously vivid writings of this officer led me immediately to forget the bleak atmosphere of the archive's reading room. They dragged me into a foreign world: they revived the attitudes and thoughts of a German general in Hitler's Wehrmacht and the events of what was, in every respect, a radical war. During many years of research on the Wehrmacht I have not found a collection of personal papers that conveys a more descriptive, more moving image of the German war in the east than Heinrici's letters and diaries. In my view Heinrici's papers are the most informative sources left by a senior member of the conservative military elite of the Third Reich.

I have analysed these prominent documents in my book *Hitlers Heerführer. Die deutschen Oberbefehlshaber im Krieg gegen die Sowjetunion 1941/42* (Oldenbourg Verlag: München, 2006; 2nd edn, 2007). In addition, I have published Heinrici's most important papers from the first year of the campaign in the east in a separate book, which was well received and soon sold out (*Ein deutscher General an der Ostfront. Die Briefe und Tagebücher des Gotthard Heinrici 1941/42*. Sutton Verlag: Erfurt, 2001). This book was and still is very important to me because of the extraordinary value of Heinrici's writings. Therefore I am all the more pleased that it is now also published in English.

As in the German edition, the selected documents date from the autumn of 1940, when preparations for Operation Barbarossa were under way, until the end of the heavy fighting in the wake of the Soviet winter offensive in May 1942. This period was the most important phase of German warfare, and even of the Second World War as a whole. During this time the German army met its fate in both military and moral terms.

Part I gives some biographical details about Heinrici and discuss his views and attitudes by referring to many additional papers written by this German general from both before and after 1941–1942. I also analyse the documents that are presented in the second part of the book. I have revised and slightly amended the text for the English edition. A substantial revision of the book was not, however, necessary – the text still stands up in the light of current research.

I am confident that the English reader will be as intrigued as I was fifteen years ago in Freiburg on the slopes of the Black Forest when I read Heinrici's papers for the first time. My reaction was astonishment, consternation, empathy, incomprehension – at any rate I was strongly drawn into them. After reading my book the great historian Fritz Stern wrote: 'Tremendously impressive and important – a moving image!'

I would like to thank Rupert Harding and Pen & Sword, Christine Brocks (translation) and Sarah Cook (editing), especially for their co-operation in making a small part of German history and historiography accessible for the English reader.

Johannes Hürter
Munich, May 2014

Tears of the Fatherland (1636)

Andreas Gryphius

transl. Michael Haldane

We have been laid to waste, to more than utter waste!
The raging bugle's blast, the troopers' savage plunder,
The battened sword in blood, the cannon's crashing thunder,
Have locusted all labour's stocks in sweating haste.
The towers stand in flames, the church is stormed and razed,
The town hall smokes in ruins, the strong lie hacked asunder,
And virgins raped. We see all over, and all under,
Fire, pestilence and death, and heart and mind are dazed.
Now through this town, these earthworks, blood is streaming fresh.
And for three times six years, our rivers flow with flesh
In shoving currents, bridled with a torpid shoal.
Nought have I said of that, more hideous than death,
More fell than flames and hunger's urge and plague's foul breath:
The countless sackings of the treasure of the soul.

'It is like the Thirty Years War, the same habits and customs. Only those who have power have any rights. I have been involved in war for six and a half years, but I have never experienced anything like this.'

Gotthard Heinrici,
19 November 1941 (doc 70)

PART I

Biography, Background and Attitudes of a Wehrmacht General

Chapter 1

Introduction

In the heated debate on the Wehrmacht's involvement in Nazi and war crimes conducted in the Soviet Union, historians have lost sight of the role of the generals. And yet, the high-ranking commanders on the Eastern Front, including army group and army commanders, corps commanders and division commanders, played a key role and determined the fate of millions of soldiers and civilians. It seems that exploring the generals' thoughts and actions is frowned upon as a 'history from above'. However, this very view from above is in fact a useful addition to the history of the 'ordinary soldier' and to micro-studies of individual units or areas.

Initially, the infantry general Gotthard Heinrici commanded an army corps, and from January 1942 onwards an army in the central sector of the Eastern Front. His private papers form one of the largest and richest sources left by any of the Wehrmacht generals.[1] Thus it is all the more surprising that Heinrici is one of the forgotten generals of the German–Soviet war.[2] His numerous, at times daily, personal notes on the course of the campaign give us a rich and authentic picture from the perspective of a senior officer, which no other corps and army commander has provided.[3]

The excerpts from Heinrici's letters and diaries published in this book date from the period when preparations for Operation Barbarossa were under way, and in particular from the first year of the eastern campaign (*Ostfeldzug*), which started with the German attack on 22 June 1941 and the advance of the Wehrmacht during that summer and autumn. This was followed by the halt before Moscow and the Soviet counteroffensive at the beginning of December, and the end of the Russian attacks in May 1942. This highly influential period pointed the way for the course of the war. It was the phase of the most significant and intense activity of the German army in the Soviet Union, which was already characterized by all the types of warfare that the later years would bring, including mobile and positional warfare, offensives and defensives, advances and retreats, the 'war of scorched earth' and partisan warfare. It was also the year in which what has been called the 'rupture of civilisation' (Dan Diner) and the war crimes started, that is to say, the radicalization of the battlefield, the mistreatment of prisoners of war, the economic exploitation of the Soviet Union, the ill-treatment of civilians and the murder of the European Jews. In this year a course was set that would have repercussions far beyond the Second World War. Apart from the disaster of Stalingrad, it is these first twelve months in particular which have shaped our remembrance of this terrible war until today, more than seventy years after the German attack on the Soviet Union. So there is a good reason for focusing on this phase of the conflict.

Heinrici's notes from the German–Soviet war are especially dense for the first year, which he spent continuously at the Eastern Front. He was aware of how crucial these events were and sought to document his part in them. The general reminded his wife several times to store and keep safe the letters, reports and diaries he was sending, because they were 'documents'.[4] It seems that he spent every free minute writing down his impressions and descriptions of his military operations. For this purpose, he used three different types of writing. Handwritten letters addressed to his wife, daily at times and interrupted for only a few days even in the most stressful periods of crisis, have survived in full. During the first half-year of the campaign he found time to keep a handwritten personal diary. Once or twice a month he sent an extensive typewritten report about the war to his family. In his diary Heinrici focuses on battles and operations, yet occasionally he gives some more general impressions. He records his war experiences and summarizes the military situation, and offers observations about the country and its people. In the letters to his wife, however, he initially concentrates on his private affairs, interrupted by short reflections on the war in general. In the course of the crisis in December 1941 he was forced to give up this extensive threefold chronicle, and had time only for letters to his wife, which gradually turned into more general reports on the mood and the military situation. This did not change even when Heinrici again took up writing his diary between January and March 1942.

From these sources have been chosen passages that give the most insight into Heinrici's perception of the war. In this context, greater emphasis has been put on observations of war, politics and the occupied territories than on descriptions of single battles and military details. It should be noted in this regard that attitudes and perceptions of war are one thing, actions and the reality of war are another. The latter remain to be examined in greater depth by drawing not only on private sources – and not only on the papers of a single general – but also on a wide range of official material.[5]

Accounts of the biography and background of this Wehrmacht general, as well as some reflections on how to contextualize the sources, precede the extracts selected from his personal record of his experiences.

Chapter 2

Life and Career

Gotthard Heinrici was born in Gumbinnen on 25 December 1886, the son of the protestant pastor Paul Heinrici.[1] He attended the *Königliches Friedrichs-Gymnasium*, a type of secondary school with strong emphasis on academic education. After his final school exams, he left his hometown in East Prussia and on 8 March 1905 entered the Royal Prussian (6th Thuringian) Infantry Regiment No. 95 in Gotha, Coburg and Hildburghausen as an officer cadet. During the First World War the young senior lieutenant filled several different positions at the front, in the rear area and at headquarters. Initially, he acquired experience at the front as a battalion and regimental adjutant, as a company and battalion commander and as a brigade adjutant during two years of mobile and positional warfare. Heinrici was involved in the battles in Belgium (August–September 1914), in East Prussia and Poland (September 1914–September 1915) and in northern France (September 1915–September 1916), including Verdun (Hill 304), and received the Iron Cross both first and second class for his efforts at the Eastern Front. After his deployment at the front, he was trained in quartermaster duties at the headquarters of several different units at the front and in the rear area in Poland, Hungary, Romania and at the Western Front. He then successfully finished the Sedan course, a programme of special training for General Staff officers lasting four weeks. Due to the war the duration of this course was reduced in time from the usual period of a year. On 28 February 1918 Heinrici was appointed as first General Staff officer of the 203rd Division on the Western Front. In this role he witnessed the turning point of the war in the 'great battle of France', from the defensive campaigns to surrender and demobilization.

Returning to East Prussia, in February 1919 Heinrici was again deployed as a General Staff officer at the General Command I in Königsberg. His further positions in the Reichswehr were: tactics instructor of General Staff officers (*Führergehilfen*) candidates from October 1920 to August 1924, company commander in Schwäbisch Gmünd (a town in the German state of Wurttemberg) from September

1924 to September 1927, officer of the army organizations branch (*Heeres-Organisationsabteilung*) at the Ministry of the Reichswehr from October 1927 to September 1930, battalion commander in Osterode/ East Prussia from October 1930 to September 1932, first General Staff officer at Group Command I in Berlin from October 1932 to January 1933 and finally head of department in the Ministry of the Reichswehr, later the War Ministry, from February 1933 to October 1937. During his career, in which he held these different positions in army units, the General Staff and the ministry, as was typical for a General Staff officer, he was promoted from captain to colonel (1 March 1933).

His promotions were more frequent during the period of Germany's rearmament and during the war. On 1 January 1936 he was appointed major general, on 1 March 1938 lieutenant general, on 1 June 1940 general of the infantry and on 1 January 1943 colonel general. This was, to be sure, a very good but not an extraordinary career; the only flaw was that he had not proved himself in combat often enough during the first two years of the Second World War. From 12 October 1937 he commanded the 16th Infantry Division, Münster/Westphalia, which was deployed in the homeland to secure the western border during the campaign in Poland. After temporarily being second in command of the VII Army Corps in February 1940, on 8 April 1940 he was appointed second in command of the XII Army Corps, which penetrated the Maginot Line south of Saarbrücken during the German invasion of western Europe.

On 18 June 1940 Heinrici became commanding general of the XXXXIII Army Corps. With this unit he advanced almost uncontested into central France (Bourges). After the armistice of 22 June he was based in the area of Le Havre–Bayeux (and later as far as Mont St Michel). It was during this period that Heinrici was involved in the preparations for Operation Sealion (*Operation Seelöwe*), that is to say, the German invasion of Great Britain. In April 1941 the General Command moved from the English Channel to Poland and took part in the offensive against the Soviet Union. This campaign put Heinrici and his corps to the test.[2] Initially as part of the 4th Army under General von Kluge, then from 4 July with the 2nd Army under General von Weichs, Heinrici's corps advanced from the Bug line north of Brest-Litovsk towards the River Berezina near Babruysk until the end of July, crossed this river and the Dnieper and paved the way for the 'cauldron of Gomel'. For this achievement, Heinrici was awarded the Knight's Cross. After being involved in the battle of Kiev, his corps was relocated to the area northwest of Bryansk at the end of September and took a leading role in the encirclement of the Bryansk front from the north. After the successful battle at Vyazma and Bryansk, the corps moved to Likhvin at the River Oka. The *rasputitsa* – the season of mud – in the second half of October brought the advance to a halt but when frost set in at the beginning of November, the offensive restarted. Heinrici's corps formed part of the 2nd Panzer Army under General Guderian, which advanced towards Tula and Moscow. After Aleksin was captured, the advance slowed down and finally collapsed on 5 December. Enemy attacks and disastrous conditions brought Heinrici's corps to the brink of destruction and forced a retreat back to Kaluga in December and to Yukhnov in January. Here, in order to prevent encirclement, a month-long ferocious battle flared up over securing the *Rollbahn*, the route taken by the German supply trucks from Brest via Minsk towards Moscow.

Protecting the *Rollbahn* was the 4th Army's most important task. Since 19 December Heinrici's corps had again been subordinated to this army, over which he himself was unexpectedly given command on 20 January 1942. The new commander proved himself arguably the most able defence expert of the central sector of the Eastern Front. First, the area around Spas Demensk, the army headquarters, had to be held against the attacks of the Red Army, which continued vigorously until May 1942. Despite numerous enemy breakthroughs and the threat of encirclement, the 4th Army accomplished this objective. During the year that followed the end of the Russian offensive, this sector of the front remained relatively quiet. But in the summer of 1943 the Red Army attacked again. The 4th Army withstood the onslaught, initially by taking up the so-called buffalo position (*Büffelstellung*) in March 1943, then the panther position (*Pantherstellung*) at Orsha, near the motorway to Moscow. However, these skilful defensive actions could only delay but not prevent the destruction of the 4th Army. In June 1944 it was defeated, together with the entire Army Group Centre (*Heeresgruppe Mitte*). Shortly beforehand, Heinrici had fallen ill, so that he was not able to command this last battle personally.

On 16 August 1944 Heinrici, recovered from his illness, was appointed commander of the 1st Panzer Army and proved himself successful in the defensive battles fought in Hungary and Moravia. Due to his extensive experience as a defence expert, on 20 March 1945 he was moved to the command of Army Group Vistula, which was given the task of stopping the Red Army's advance on Berlin. Yet this was too much of a challenge even for Heinrici. On 29 April, after the collapse of the front on the River Oder and dissensions within the Supreme Command of the Armed Forces (*Oberkommando der Wehrmacht, OKW*), he was removed from command at his own request. He escaped to Schleswig-Holstein, but was taken prisoner by British troops in Flensburg on 28 May. In May 1948 he returned to Germany. Gotthard Heinrici died on 10 December 1971 in Karlsruhe.

Chapter 3

Heinrici's Character

To understand the German generals' conduct during the war against the Soviet Union, a certain disposition has to be taken into account, which was the result of a specific kind of socialization in Wilhelmine Germany during the First World War and the interwar years. In medical parlance, 'disposition' means the liability or tendency to suffer from a certain illness and represents an essential part of aetiology. Accordingly, the historian has to examine the predispositions resulting in the fact that the Wehrmacht generals, as a traditional, conservative elite, not only accepted but also supported Nazi war policy and warfare, which went far beyond traditional boundaries and committed terrible crimes. Their backgrounds, careers and experiences shaped the generals' political and military mindset, which crucially influenced their view of dictatorship and war.[1] In this book we can only make some general comments, which should encourage a better understanding of the documents that follow and the mentality of a high-ranking army commander at the Eastern Front. A number of typical features can, however, be found in Heinrici's biography.

In common with most of the generals who in June 1941 commanded a corps, an army or an army group in the Soviet Union, Heinrici was born in the 1880s as a protestant Prussian. A member of the upper social strata supporting the state, he shared some key features of his background with other generals: birth and property, the spirit of bureaucracy and military, Church and a special education. His father was a protestant pastor in East Prussia, who later advanced to the position of a general superintendent. During the First World War Heinrici's father joined the Pan-German League, an ultra-nationalist organization founded in 1891, 'with the deepest patriotic conviction'.[2] Until his final school exams, Heinrici spent his early years in Gumbinnen, a garrison town with a high number of civil servants. The provincial milieu of the agrarian area at the border with Russia shaped his early political socialization. Heinrici himself described these influences as conservative, national, monarchistic, faithful to the Church and, due to the lack of any industry, far away from any socialist ideas.[3] In addition, he was influenced by anti-Slav resentments and the latent anti-Semitism that was common among clerics in East Elbia. A crucial concern in the region was the 'Russian Menace' (*Russengefahr*), which lingered in Heinrici's memory as distinctly as the lithograph 'Peoples of Europe, protect your most sacred possessions', designed by Wilhelm II, which hung in Heinrici's school assembly hall. Although this was in fact aimed at the 'Yellow Peril' during the Boxer Rebellion in China, it also included a reference to 'half-Asian' Russia.[4]

The next two crucial periods in Heinrici's life were his years of training in the Imperial army and his experience of war and revolution between 1914 and 1919. Military training in the Prussian army confirmed his conservative and monarchistic views and even added an elitist class consciousness. However, these military and political values gained during times of peace were seriously challenged during war and revolution. The First World War was a pivotal experience for Heinrici and his generation of officers.[5] He witnessed modern warfare in its confusing complexity on all the fronts in the west and east. Three aspects in particular were crucial for his later deployment in the Soviet Union.

In September 1914 Heinrici was confronted with that spectre from his childhood, the 'Russian Menace', when his regiment was involved in pursuing Russian troops retreating from East Prussia. In the liberated East Prussian territories he found 'vivid images of rampant and senseless destruction, which we have never considered possible'; it was a shocking experience that reinforced his resentment against the barbarian Russians.[6] When he crossed the Russian border and advanced to the village of Wladyslawow, these feelings became even stronger.[7] 'What we found in terms of "kultura" was deeply shocking. Kaftan Jews with ringlets, small dirty houses, shops with wooden window shutters and crudely painted pictures of the offered goods (because customers were illiterate), no pavements; to cut the matter short: that was not what we expected coming to Russia.' He did not change his mind about the brave but 'primitive' Russian, the backwardness of Slav culture and the inhospitable character of the country[8] during his combat missions in Poland in the following months and years.

Heinrici saw that the horror of modern warfare was not limited to combatants but also affected civilians in the rear areas, and he had direct experience of this in his homeland, East Prussia. As a supply officer in Romania in 1917 he was faced with the fundamental problems of occupation politics. He was particularly struck by the sometimes disastrous food situation in villages crowded with refugees. To be sure, Heinrici expressed moral concerns when the occupation power decided to separate the women and children refugees from the men in one of the villages and to transport them elsewhere. However, ultimately he justified this decision. 'It means to rob the family of its breadwinner, to send them into the unknown, and to keep the men. For the people, that is very cruel. If it were our own countrymen, we would probably call it barbaric. Yet we need the male workforce to till the fields in spring. These lads can work some acres, which will help the people at home. That is all that matters, even if it means that some Romanian women and children go down.'[9]

In this illuminating diary entry, Heinrici describes a street where, some days before, several civilians froze to death. 'One cannot at all compare this war with the Thirty Years War. In terms of destruction the latter was child's play in contrast to the present war.' Heinrici's reference to the Thirty Years War emphasized how the current conflict had relapsed into a form of warfare from days gone by. This new type of war was no longer defined by exercises and drilling on parade grounds and then fighting in straight battle lines as was traditional in Wilhelmine Germany. Instead it was an industrial and technological war of attrition which swallowed up the resources of the homeland and, as compensation, exploited the occupied territories with no regard for foreign civilians.[10] Heinrici himself called this kind of warfare 'barbarism', yet he accepted the transformation from traditional 'cabinet' wars[11] to the 'total' war of the people despite the discomfort and indignation he initially felt in 1914 when he was still in East Prussia. The First World War was already more brutal in the hinterland of the Eastern Front than in the west and – despite the differences between the world wars – this foreshadowed what happened there during the Second World War.

The connection between the front, the rear areas and the homeland is also crucial for the third aspect of Heinrici's experiences. As for all the officers of the Imperial army, the collapse of Imperial Germany, which led to capitulation, revolution and republic, meant the end of Heinrici's world. As early as mid-October 1918 he expected a revolution 'along the lines of Russia'[12] and deplored 'that in only a few days, while we were out there in battle without noticing anything, our old fatherland collapsed. What is upon us? A clique of Jews and

Socialists now rule and they only care about the International.'[13] Conveniently, a scapegoat had already been found. Even in old age, Heinrici was indignant about the 'stab-in-the-back' and about socialist subversion, which started in the homeland, spread to the rear areas and eventually infected the combat troops.[14] 'We were shocked! All our fighting, our victories, our sacrifices and deaths for Germany – all in vain! The Social Democrats finished off the Empire of Bismarck by stabbing it in the back. ... Instead of calling up a united Germany in these hard times, they started off a class struggle.'

'Bolshevism' was not only a threat from within, but also from outside. After his unit was demobilized, in early 1919 Heinrici rushed to Königsberg to defend his East Prussian home country against the Poles and 'Bolshevist hordes' who were supposed to be advancing from the Baltic states.[15] This battle never took place. However, Heinrici was immediately deployed at the General Command of Königsberg. On 3 March 1919 he took part in quelling the Republican Army and Naval Defence Troops (*Republikanische Armee und Marine-Volkswehr*), revolutionary units that had been established in Königsberg during the uprising of 29 November 1918. In addition, he organized border patrol units and planned the recapture of Poznan. These and similar actions were stopped when the Versailles Treaty was signed on 28 June 1919 as they were contrary to the policies of the Reich government.[16] Heinrici remained convinced that he should stand in the front line against Bolshevism and 'Slavdom', which in East Prussia was considered an equal threat.

For Heinrici's generation and profession, the First World War was a traumatic experience which had repercussions in the decades leading up to the Second World War and beyond. It was clear that modern wars could not be fought on the same basis as wars in the past because a huge effort would be required from the entire population. Military leaders were uneasy about this extension of warfare. The First World War had also shown that modern conflict had evolved into a form of uncontrollable and devastating warfare, and that the limited warfare of eighteenth- and nineteenth-century Europe was a thing of the past. The younger officers in particular were less likely to question these developments.

The demands of this new form of warfare were also bound to have profound repercussions in political terms. Firstly, they justified using any possible advantage, in particular the exploitation of occupied territories, especially if their inhabitants were considered 'inferior'.

Secondly, only an authoritarian government could be trusted to unite and to organize the entire nation for battle. The disaster of late 1918 had led military leaders to believe that a stable home front was absolutely vital for the war effort. To achieve this, a united *Volksgemeinschaft*[17] and the ability to take drastic steps to put down any looming protests behind the front lines were required. Jews and Socialists were blamed for breaching the *Burgfrieden* – a term used for the political truce between the SPD, the trade unions and the government in order to support the war effort. Given the events in Russia, the emphasis on a united people always had an 'anti-Bolshevik' subtext, mingled with older, traditional resentments against Social Democrats, Jews and Russians. Thus, during the First World War and the turbulent years that followed, the acceptance of 'total war' was combined in a dangerous way with militant anti-Bolshevism, anti-Semitism and anti-Slavism. This combination would end in a catastrophe of unforeseen dimensions in the next world war.

In the political system of the post-war era many Germans were susceptible to totalitarian and revanchist ideas. The internal and external weaknesses of the republic were as unbearable for monarchist and nationalist officers as the existence of some of the states established by what Heinrici called 'the corrupt peoples' of Eastern Europe.[18] It was a matter of course for Heinrici, who championed the right-wing German National People's Party (*Deutschnationale Volkspartei*, DNVP), to support key objectives such as authoritarian reforms and border changes, especially in the east. In March 1920 he and his General Command in Königsberg supported the Kapp putsch.[19] This, however, did not affect his career in a negative way.

After this episode Heinrici no longer interfered in domestic politics. It should be noted in this context that few concepts have caused so much misunderstanding as the notion of an 'unpolitical Reichswehr'. Groener's and von Schleicher's pro-republican orientation and Seeckt's *attentisme* had a lot of political influence. The military elite were by no means willing to give up their social and political position, which they had gained during the Wilhelmine period. Very few of the military elite had direct political influence at that time, and this situation had not changed under the republic. Yet it is also fair to assume that only a few officers failed to take any interest in domestic and foreign politics, and did not play at least a small social and political role. Besides, as a modern General Staff officer in the Ministry of Defence, it was Heinrici's professional duty to take into account social and economic as well as political affairs. Strategy and politics are inseparable. After 1945 the generals tried to justify their conduct during the Nazi period by suggesting they had been trained to be 'non-political soldiers' in the Reichswehr, focusing exclusively on military business. Heinrici's letters from the time when he was a member of the Reichswehr prove the opposite. They demonstrate his deep interest in politics. Particularly in 1932–3, during the transition period from democracy to dictatorship, his letters are full of extended reflections about the political situation and give detailed insights into his views on National Socialism.

Heinrici was strictly opposed to Weimar's party democracy, its pluralism and political divisions. Instead, he championed an authoritarian state, but he would have accepted a more moderate version than the Third Reich. He welcomed Brüning's attempt to invite all political parties and social organizations to cooperate. Military considerations played an important role in his thoughts, as shown by his disappointment when the DNVP stopped President Hindenburg from serving a second term at the beginning of 1932, which caused further protests.[20] 'Hindenburg and the government only wish to create a *Volksgemeinschaft* against the French and the Poles. When they invade Germany we cannot tell the Socialists: You are not allowed to fight because you are not a member of the DNVP. Our representatives in Geneva do not require a political group but the people behind them during their negotiations. Yet this very situation has already occurred.' At that time Heinrici still supported the 'sensible right', whereas he did not approve of the 'radicalism of the Nazis'.[21]

Yet when conservative governments under von Papen and von Schleicher failed to create a *Volksgemeinschaft* essential to support the Reichswehr's extensive plans for rearmament, Heinrici changed his views. Great expectations merged with scepticism in his comments when Hitler took over the government. Heinrici would have preferred a cabinet of the DNVP supported by the NSDAP.[22] However, the very first steps of the new government strengthened his hopes 'that we have finished with the Marxian Jewish pigsty'.[23] He predicted, without expressing an opinion, that:[24] 'The next years will certainly be very exciting and later on also years of war.'

Heinrici's comments on the swift establishment of Nazi rule illustrate a rather insecure political viewpoint, typical of his overall attitude during the Third Reich. This officer, shaped by the norms and values of Wilhelmine Germany, which were shaken and damaged during the revolution and the post-war period, was not non-political but politically unstable. On the one hand he was impressed, even enthusiastic, about the radical changes in Germany; on the other he criticized the new policies where they were arbitrary and excessive.[25] Heinrici was well aware of the new and revolutionary character of the political situation and very early on used the phrase 'dictatorship' to describe the increasingly dominant position of the NSDAP.[26] Yet this nationalist conservative officer was more than willing to ignore his unease over some of Hitler's radical measures and the marginalization of the other parties in the coalition in order to support the 'great objective of again turning Germany into a nation state'.[27] With satisfaction he observed the end of the Weimar republic, 'the years under Social Democratic rule',[28] and saw the 'communist lice' leaving Germany.[29] He considered this turning point as a successful revenge on the political right for the events of 1918–19. Accordingly, he was pleased about the public demonstrations of Germany's new unity by displaying the black-red-white flag, the colours of Imperial Germany, and the swastika.[30]

As a military expert, first and foremost he hoped the new government would overcome the trauma of 1918, the combination of national discord and military weakness, and would be able to create a united nation ready to go to war. In view of France's dominant position in the European system, Heinrici forecast that:[31] 'Only when Hitler has militarized the entire German people – and that is what his political agenda is about, even the Reich Labour Service serves this purpose – and when we are a power nation again, change is possible. If there is another war sometime in the future, one thing is for sure: we won't see any defeatists as we did fifteen years ago. The Nazis will sort that out. They will know how to lead the people.'

Ultimately, Heinrici's delight in view of the new 'national' domestic and military policies prevailed over his unease about the radical nature of the new regime. Nothing shows this more clearly than his views on the anti-Semitic measures, which he carefully observed. His anti-Semitism had probably developed at an early stage and was consolidated by his experiences of 'Jewish Bolshevism'. In connection with his Christian conservative values, this mindset led to some peculiar argumentative leaps. In March 1933 he regretfully gave an account of the physical abuse of a 'good' Jew he was acquainted with. At the same time he justified the incident by referring to the situation in 1919 'when we returned back home and sailors with red armbands ruled'.[32] He welcomed the removal of Jewish civil servants and doctors from service.[33] 'I have never condemned the Jews in general, but it is the best to limit them to their original position. The same applies to the Centre Party. Apparently, the wind of change is already blowing in our schools.' Yet he considered pogroms and boycotts of Jewish businesses on 1 April 1933 as a 'very unfortunate step, which will cause insults and injustice'.[34] 'It was necessary to force the Jews out of their influential positions. Yet the means was inappropriate.' However, a few days later he emphasized 'the greatness [of the time]', justified 'necessary' sanctions and mandatory measures, 'even some hardships', and praised Hitler and Goebbels:[35] 'They carried out the boycott against Jews with great skill!' Some time later, when he got hold of an exiled newspaper printed in Amsterdam, by his own account he learned what 'atrocity propaganda' meant and took the opportunity to justify Nazi policies:[36] 'If the Jews are represented by people like this, they deserve what they get.'

As the Nazi *Judenpolitik* grew more radical, Heinrici's comments on the topic became less frequent and more cautious. Yet although he was opposed to the pogrom on 9 November 1938,[37] the disenfranchisement and persecution of German Jews, which he was well aware of, did not affect his view of the Nazi regime. In January 1939 Heinrici, then a divisional commander, attended an NSDAP event in Detmold[38] as guest of honour and heard a speech by Alfred Rosenberg,[39] which left no room for doubt about the aim of Nazi anti-Semitism.[40] 'For an hour he talked about the horrible Jews. The Jewish question, he said, would only be solved when there were no more Jews in Germany. The Nazis would do everything to accomplish that. Anyway, it would be best if there weren't any Jews left in the whole of Europe.'

For Heinrici the pivotal issues were national and military revival and a common sense of purpose between the Wehrmacht and the people.[41] As a department head in the Ministry of the Reichswehr responsible for recruitment and replacements, he had to address controversial issues such as *Wehrertüchtigung* (pre-military training for the Hitler Youth) and the relationship of the ministry to the troops. In this context the ideal of a *Volksgemeinschaft* was, for Heinrici, the foundation of a dynamic military policy. He welcomed it when the SA, formerly a competitor of the army, fell from power.[42] In the aftermath of these developments, he tried to build up a soldiers' league (*Soldatenbund*), a military organization for retiring reservists standing apart from party politics.[43] Heinrici fully realized the potential of a militarized people under a totalitarian regime. When in his public speeches he highlighted the *Wehrwille* of young Germans, that is to say, their willingness to fight, as the basis of their common ideology which he considered a decisive advantage in comparison with the First World War, this was much more than just a verbal concession to the regime.[44] It does not simply reflect a careerist's opportunism, but rather it is the attitude of an officer who endorsed the political system. He was convinced of its military and political advantages, impressed by the 'new spirit'[45] and willing to ignore his objections to it, especially those concerning Nazi racial and church policies.[46]

Accordingly, Heinrici's reaction to the Blomberg–Fritsch crisis and its impact on the Wehrmacht leaders was moderate. He attributed Blomberg's downfall to his 'hubris', while he regretted the end of Fritsch's career. In general he remarked:[47] 'The new men are very capable and efficient. They are ready to do everything for the cause. Anyway, the crisis is resolved in the best possible way and we are happy that the situation has been solved in a rather skilful fashion.' Although not a National Socialist himself, from the summer of 1933 onwards Heinrici would remain more than just a loyal servant to the Nazi state so long as the new regime did what he expected it to do:[48] 'In military terms we benefit from the new government enormously. Its support of all military interests leaves nothing to be desired.' Even Hitler's hazardous foreign policy did not change Heinrici's generally positive view of the Nazi regime. In September 1938 he was extremely concerned about the danger of a European war,[49] because 'we are not yet strong enough to cope with this challenge'. However, Hitler's highly successful foreign policy reduced the risk.[50] Incidents such as the Blomberg–Fritsch crisis, the Sudeten crisis and the 'Crystal Night' (*Reichskristallnacht*) did not turn Heinrici into an opponent of the regime, although several other nationalist, conservative generals began to have their doubts.[51] Apparently, Hitler's personal influence on the generals did not fail in Heinrici's case. At the beginning of 1939 Heinrici witnessed the first of Hitler's two extended speeches addressing German generals, when he openly promoted his ideological and political objectives.[52] Shortly afterwards, Heinrici gave a speech on Hitler's 50th birthday before the staff of his division in which he praised not only the Fuehrer's political success, but also his 'infinite love for the German people whose *Lebensraum*[53] and liveability are his highest task'.[54] This again was not just a rhetorical bow to the regime.

On the contrary, the speech shows the extent of Heinrici's commitment to Nazi dictatorship. Although he did not fully comprehend the radical nature of the aggressive Nazi ideology, and even felt uneasy about some aspects of it, he appreciated that it would allow him to fulfil his own political and military aims.

Heinrici's fascination for the new regime even grew during the first year of the war. In no way did he blame Hitler and his policy of aggression. Instead he considered it a pre-emptive war – fully in line with the traditional phobia of encirclement dating from Wilhelmine times – 'which by all means we would be forced to fight later on anyway'.[55] After the invasion of Poland, he blamed Great Britain for continuing the war in order to defend its 'world dominating position', which was threatened by Germany.[56] At the same time Heinrici was carried away by the victories of the Nazis. Before 1939 he used to be cautious when it came to issues of foreign politics. During the war, however, he was gripped by the idea of German hegemony. When German troops occupied Denmark and Norway, he saw that the objective was 'to turn the Scandinavian states into satellite states of the Greater German Reich'.[57] 'The Fuehrer's decision to seize them is of Napoleonic quality: great and daring.' At that time it was common to think in these ambitious terms.

The successful campaign in the west excited Heinrici's 'admiration for a government which succeeded in fighting all our enemies, individually and one after another, starting with Austria, the Czechs, the Polish etc so that we could always gather our forces at one crucial point.'[58] With great satisfaction Heinrici observed France's defeat, which he thought was caused by the degenerate state of the French people brought on by their 'racial mixture'. He believed it was crucial to weaken the traditional enemy deeply and for a long time.[59]

At the end of the first year of war Heinrici was frustrated at being kept in the 'second line' during a successful campaign and desperately waited for a more challenging deployment.[60] Despite all his enthusiasm for the German victories he recognized the problems of the war situation after the campaign in France, in particular the difficulty 'finding the right time to finish' (doc 1). According to Heinrici, the most crucial and difficult challenge Germany was facing, with her weak navy, was to defeat the main enemy, England, in the battle over 'world prestige' (*Weltgeltung*).[61] Occupying Turkey, invading Asia Minor and making a foray to the Suez Canal were for him possible actions that would shake the British position – by agreement with the Soviet Union.[62]

At an early stage Heinrici realized that there was yet another option: turning against the Soviet Union for strategic and ideological reasons (doc 1). The comparison with Napoleon suggests that he felt rather uncomfortable with this option. A year earlier Heinrici had been in favour of the Hitler–Stalin Pact[63] and even concluded:[64] 'It has always been to their benefit when Germany and Russia stood together.' Despite all long-standing hostilities between the two countries, he recognized Russia's power and the potential danger of challenging Germany's eastern neighbour (doc 3). So it is fair to assume that Heinrici started his deployment in the east with excitement, nervousness and misgivings.

These attitudes, which in part already existed before 1914 in a latent form and developed throughout the First World War and the periods of revolution, republic and dictatorship that followed, are listed below, using Heinrici as an example, since they are crucial for understanding a senior front commander and his views on the war against the Soviet Union. This analysis stresses Heinrici's stance as an individual and shows that his outlook was typical. As an officer, Heinrici's experiences from the beginning of the First World War to the eve of Operation Barbarossa were characterized by:

1. Consolidation of anti-Slavism, anti-Semitism and anti-Socialism. Heinrici's service as an officer on the Eastern Front during the First World War reinforced his contempt for the allegedly inferior Slav people. According to him 'Jewish bolshevism' proved a 'deadly foe' in times of defeat and revolution. Social Democracy, the 'Jewish Marxism', was to blame for the downfall of the German Empire and the weakness of the Weimar Republic.
2. Radicalization of the military doctrine. Military leaders saw the First World War not as a conflict limited to their own soldierly profession but as a struggle for the survival of an entire people and their way of life. This social Darwinistic concept of war served to justify the uncompromising use of all resources against the enemy. Moral concerns and traditional values receded in favour of the 'necessities of war'.
3. Tendency towards a totalitarian state. The new dimension of war as a struggle of the people emphasized the necessity of the

unity, which was missing in the final phase of the First World War. Neither a monarchistic nor a republican system had been able to create a militarized *Volksgemeinschaft*. Consequently, the totalitarian option became even more attractive. The *wehrfreudige* ('war-hungry') Nazi rule not only successfully applied strict leadership and a policy of rearmament, it also offered the traditional elites the chance to fulfil their political aims.

4. Extension of foreign policy objectives. The foreign policy achievements of the Nazi regime and the unexpected gain of power during the first two years of the war affected even cautious generals and prompted them to adjust their standards of success. They were hoping first for an amendment of the Versailles Treaty, second, for the realization of their longstanding dream of a Greater German Empire, and finally for 'bold' power politics of the sort pursued by Alexander the Great or Napoleon.

Of course this mindset did not apply to all the officers of Heinrici's generation, but it is safe to assume that exceptions were rare. The effect of these attitudes on their conduct during the German–Soviet war must now be examined.

Chapter 4

War Images

In October 1947 Heinrici, who was at that time a prisoner of war in a British camp, was taken to Nuremberg to be questioned in the context of the pending trial of senior generals ('OKW-trial'). When the American investigating officer Walter Rapp asked him about the military and political aspects of his view of the Nazi regime in 1941, he answered that during the war 'military aspects were self-evidently more important because that was what life was about. I have confined myself to these things. As a corps commander I myself was nothing more than a soldier. Consequently I was fully committed to the military performance of my men, to see our task through. I did everything for my men.'[1] In the course of questioning Heinrici also pointed out that, during the first weeks of the invasion of Russia, 'we had to march between 12 and 15 hours and that we were always in combat. Mr Rapp, you have to put yourself in our position and try to understand. We were under constant pressure due to continuous combat operations causing extreme physical and mental exertion.'

Heinrici's answers mirror the stereotypical defence strategy of German generals after the war who were determined to avoid the inconvenient and, given the potential legal consequences, dangerous questions of the investigating Allied authorities. However, it would be simplistic to dismiss his arguments for this reason. Undoubtedly, and for obvious motives, defendants often bent the truth in their statements after the war. But to treat all their statements as lies would be to ignore the different degrees of honesty, from gross falsehoods to half-truths to genuine statements. Accordingly, we have to verify and assess, in a nuanced way and on the basis of historical documents, his claim that he was a military commander focusing narrowly on military matters. Regardless of whether his statement was wholly true or not, it illustrates a crucial aspect of the generals' situation during the war. It highlights the simple but often ignored fact that commanders on the Eastern Front had to accomplish a professional task under extremely difficult circumstances. They were in combat, and what they did and thought has to be seen in this context, with all its challenges, problems and peculiarities.

It is a cardinal error in discussions of the Wehrmacht to take single orders and incidents out of context and examine them as if in a vacuum. As we have seen, when analysing the mental dispositions of the generals it is vital to investigate not only the pre-war and war years but also the Wilhelmine period and especially the First World War. It is equally important not to pick out and generalize from a few pieces of evidence in order to answer the question of how important the generals' role was in relation to the unquestioned war without limits that the German–Soviet conflict turned into, as well as breaches of law and war crimes. The fashionable scholarly term 'contextualization' would make sense here if conditions and circumstances are taken into consideration to a greater extent. This approach offers new possibilities to modern military historiography and should help to do justice to the complexity of the historical events.

Heinrici's letters and diaries are an excellent source of material for this contextual approach, at least in excerpts, thanks to the direct and private character of these rare autobiographical accounts by a senior front-line general. Obviously, some limitations are inevitable, due to the focus on a single person, the necessity to select documents and the nature of the source itself. Only a few out of many letters, reports and diary entries from 1941–1942 can be presented here. Numerous descriptions of combat and accounts of mostly private matters have been omitted, while non-military observations and reports on the mood at the front are favoured. The selection in this book aims to offer a representative overview of all the relevant aspects of Heinrici's perception and interpretation of the war. The same applies to the documents in terms of their relevance. Undoubtedly, it would be desirable to compare Heinrici's personal view on the war with objective facts and to add autobiographical accounts of other commanders and official army documents, but this cannot be done within the confines of this volume. Heinrici's private papers were addressed to his family or were meant as a personal record. It is impossible to know what he deliberately omitted. However, it is striking that his descriptions of wartime events are so unrestrained and that he did not shy away from criticizing the supreme leadership. Apparently Heinrici was not frightened that his letters were opened by censors, partly because many of them reached the homeland by private delivery. Therefore it is fair to assume that his papers are relatively uncensored private accounts, which increases their value as a source. So this selection of his documents contributes to understanding the relationship between an individual's attitudes, his personal view of the war and the overall conduct of it, despite the reservations that have already been mentioned.

The documents refute Heinrici's claim, quoted above, about the exclusively military workload that was forced on him by the everyday pressures of the war. However, at the same time they show a grain of truth. Certainly Heinrici was not the non-political 'only a soldier' exclusively occupied by his military tasks. His autobiographical accounts reveal a strong interest in non-military issues and in how they interacted with the war. Yet it is noticeable that these interests were superseded again and again by the latest military problems in his zone of command and finally disappeared completely in the winter crisis of 1941/2. During the mobile warfare of the first few months, when Heinrici was a commanding general, he had the time to reflect on political and other issues. As an army commander with extended responsibilities, he was caught in a fierce defensive fight during the winter months and had to focus completely on the military crisis. Heinrici himself describes how he lived in this world of war and how he excluded everything else from it (doc 105). It seems that the responsibility for an army under severe pressure made Heinrici focus narrowly on military issues – an attitude he later claimed to be true also for the time before, when he was a general commanding a smaller formation.

The professional tasks of a senior military officer were the frame of reference for his everyday work. Heinrici commanded a combination of units which could conduct independent combat missions and was self-sustaining for a certain period of time.[2] He was one of a small and elite group of senior Wehrmacht officers that included commanders of divisions (the smallest of these units), corps commanders, army commanders and finally army group commanders. At these four different levels of responsibility they were in charge of three basic aspects of warfare:[3] tactics (battle management), operations (combining several tactical actions and including long-range movements and battles) and strategy (combining all relevant aspects of tactics and operations towards an overall war aim). Further responsibilities regarding occupation policies will be discussed later.

In the conduct of operations a divisional commander was restricted to tactical aspects. Corps commanders were also primarily involved in tactical issues, but were in a position also to have an impact on operational command. An army commander led operations in his zone of command according to the guidelines of the overall strategy, and the same applies to the commander of an army group. Due to his higher level of responsibilities, the latter had to have detailed knowledge of strategic aims that a person in his position as highest-ranking commanding officer was most likely to influence. However, the overall strategy remained the responsibility of the supreme leadership, that is to say, of Hitler and – at a lower level – his immediate military advisers. Yet this did not mean that front generals ignored operational and strategic problems. Even though not every ordinary soldier of the German army carried a marshal's baton in his knapsack – to quote Napoleon – every General Staff officer who was trained in strategy did, and most of the senior leaders came from the General Staff.

The purpose of the German campaign against the Soviet Union was one of the most significant general strategic issues. Even though he was only a corps commander with limited scope, Heinrici addressed this question. Unlike the commander-in-chief and leading General Staff officers of army groups and armies who were present at a notorious meeting with Hitler on 30 March 1941, the generals of lower rank were not personally informed by Hitler about his political intentions. Yet at an early stage Heinrici got the gist of it (doc 1): the extermination of Germany's major potential enemy in continental Europe and of the Bolshevik ideology in order to focus on the war in the west. It is interesting that Heinrici knew the relevant paragraphs from Hitler's *Mein Kampf* and that he took these remarks seriously. A day before the offensive started he noted two additional objectives: the fight against the USA and the creation of an autarkic Europe by conquering and exploiting agrarian areas in the east (doc 13). Heinrici mentioned these essential war aims in a matter-of-fact way and without assessing or commenting on them. There is no sign in his writing of enthusiasm for the campaign to come, only barely suppressed scepticism. His longstanding antipathy towards Russia and his fundamental opposition to Bolshevism did not make him blind to the enormous risks of campaigning against this huge country. His scepticism became obvious later on (doc 33) and in hindsight he convincingly claimed that as early as the spring of 1941 he had considered the war against the Soviet Union a mistake (doc 3; *see* notes).

It is all the more remarkable that Heinrici repeatedly let himself get carried away by great political objectives. For him, both economic exploitation (doc 36) and destroying Bolshevism (doc 27), as well as dismembering the enemy state (doc 41), were desirable aims. On 11 December, after the Soviet counteroffensive before Moscow had started, he approvingly noted his Russian interpreter's suggestion about how to solve the 'problem of Russia': protectorates over the Baltic states; Belarus and the Ukraine should be exploited as colonial countries; the rest of the Soviet Union should be split up into republics without sovereignty; the territory reaching to Lake Baikal should be controlled by Germany, the region beyond this area controlled by Japan (doc 82). These objectives were congruent with Hitler's, and his hegemonic ambitions did not differ in the slightest from those of most of the other generals. In his private papers Heinrici is clear about the steps that would need to be taken to fulfil this policy: the elimination of Poland, the continual weakening of France, the destruction and dissolution of the Soviet Union, then a European war against England and the USA under German supremacy. Heinrici, as a typical conservative officer, was now thinking big in regard to the 'New Order' in the east – bigger even than the German military elite of 1918, whose goals were nothing like so ambitious after the peace treaty of Brest-Litovsk.

However, Heinrici's general approval of the ambitious German plans was counteracted by his doubts about whether Germany would be strong enough to complete the strategic tasks necessary to achieve them. In the course of the invasion of the Soviet Union his misgivings grew and he became increasingly critical. Apparently he never believed in a swift German success in the first place. As a trained infantry officer, he was daunted by the sheer size of the Soviet Union, which a panzer general might not have feared so much. As early as mid-July 1941 Heinrici had the frightening feeling that, even if Moscow were to be conquered, the war would continue 'from elsewhere in this vast, endless country' (doc 24). From this moment onwards, the gloomy prospect of a war lasting for many years appeared again and again in his letters and diaries, and was reinforced by the arduous experience of the German advance. Soon he criticized the military leadership for wasting precious time with prolonged debates about operational targets and with repeated changes in the strategic focus. Further points of his criticism were: underestimating the enemy, the size of the country, adverse weather conditions, insufficient provisions and clothing, inadequate logistics and exhausting the soldiers.

This criticism intensified following the crisis before Moscow. On 24 December Heinrici mentioned for the first time a sense of foreboding that Germany might be defeated (doc 91). At the same time his confidence in the supreme leadership – for the first time even in Hitler – declined, even though Heinrici still referred to him as 'the Fuehrer'. Yet it is obvious that Heinrici doubted Hitler's perception of reality and the purpose of his *Haltebefehl*.[4] Certainly Heinrici's papers from the months of crisis between December 1941 and May 1942 illustrate that he became increasingly disillusioned about the outcome of the German–Soviet war after this first setback. However, this by no means led him and the majority of generals to fundamentally oppose the overall strategy or even the Nazi regime.

The reason why Heinrici did not come to this obvious conclusion was his continuing approval of at least some of the aims of National Socialism. We can assume that his narrow-minded sense of soldierly duty, the pressure of his tasks at the front and the related sense of responsibility for the soldiers entrusted to him were further motives. Heinrici's official duties did not include reflections on strategy and politics but were primarily focused on tactical command. Even during his time as an army commander fighting on the defensive he was not in a position to take any important operational decisions.[5] It goes without saying that Heinrici, like every general, was eager to achieve military success. Yet this ambition did not diminish his duty of care towards his soldiers – he was determined not to incur unnecessary sacrifices and to avoid using them as cannon fodder. Only once did Heinrici complain about his troops and their decreasing commitment (doc 24). Otherwise his texts show that he respected and even admired the ordinary soldiers for their achievements. They also give an insight into the suffering and dying of these young men, who were abused by a criminal regime. Most of them were children at the time of the Nazi seizure of power; while some of them were responsible for the regime's crimes, they were more often its victims.

As an infantry general Heinrici was in close contact with his troops, perhaps closer than artillery or panzer generals who were more concerned with materiel and technology. His accommodation and provisions might have been better than those the ordinary *Landser* (infantrymen) had to make do with, yet he had to endure the rigours of war just like them and therefore was able to relate to their ordeal. Heinrici was constantly on the move, either in the *Kübelwagen*[6] or in the *Fieseler Storch*.[7] He comforted his exhausted, tired, sweating or freezing, lice-ridden and starving troops and was often at the very front line.[8] Particularly when he was a commanding general he had a good connection with his troops – traditionally a Prussian–German ideal.[9]

The constant confrontation with the reality of war and the front-line soldiers' suffering, which he powerfully described in his writings, was a gruelling burden for Heinrici and an additional reason for focusing even harder on his immediate military tasks the more this burden increased. As a senior officer he was under tremendous pressure to meet expectations from both above and below and to find a balance between the obligation to succeed and the need to protect his soldiers. During the advance he speculated that the infantry might soon cease to be a key part of the army. Yet in the long months of defensive battles at Moscow he realized that this branch was playing a vital role in the fighting. Entrusted with more responsibility and confronted with greater pressure, Heinrici was put to the test in this campaign.

When Heinrici was appointed an army commander, he was almost relieved to be suddenly 'pulled out of the thick of the battle' (doc 98). Yet he soon realized the nearly unbearable burden of the higher position, as his letters demonstrate. When he was still a corps commander he had criticized his superiors Kluge (Army Group Centre) and Kübler (4th Army) for refusing his proposal to retreat out of fear 'of the highest authority' (doc 96). Now he himself was under obligation to do his best in view of both the overall situation and the fate of his army. Heinrici resolutely championed the concept of mobile defence, a special tactical strategy highly developed in the German army especially, which he considered more effective and efficient than area defence. He did not shy away from standing up for his inconvenient wishes to shorten the front line by evasive movements, doing so, for instance, at a meeting on 28 February 1942 in the Fuehrer's headquarters (doc 111). In this respect he met his responsibility as an army commander without fear of disadvantaging his career. Yet these small victories against his superiors and the 'highest authority' did not relieve the tension between expectation and reality. As an army commander Heinrici remained close to the centre of events – unlike his superior, the commander-in-chief, whom Heinrici sometimes almost envied (doc 107). At the end of the months of crisis and after nearly a year of continuous service at the front he was 'worn out' by 'the imbalance between expectations from above and the reality of war' (doc 133). We should not lose sight of the immense strains that were imposed on a senior officer with his immediate responsibilities.

Heinrici's exemplary attitude towards his soldiers contrasted strongly with his judgement and treatment of the enemy. It is in this very aspect that the war in the east differed from a 'normal' war, that is to say, traditional ways of warfare were abandoned in favour of an approach that broke every norm. This leads to the discussion of the criminal character of this campaign. Heinrici's writings are particularly valuable in this respect. Not only do they shed light on the thoughts of a senior officer and his expertise in military strategy, operations and tactics, they also provide insights into the issue of a warfare without boundaries (*Entgrenzung des Krieges*) by outlining Heinrici's view of the war and the enemy. Again, this applies in particular to the first half of the year of the campaign rather than to the months of desperate defensive battles.

Already during the very first weeks Heinrici's preconceived view of the enemy got stronger.[10] For him the Red Army soldiers 'looked rather Chinese than Russian' (doc 15), were 'deceitful' (doc 14), 'devious' (doc 15), 'dishonest' (doc 24) and 'glued to the terrain like lice' (doc 36), and behaved 'like a beast towards our injured soldiers' (doc 18). Heinrici tolerated and even justified German soldiers who reacted by 'clean[ing] up among them [enemy soldiers] on various occasions without mercy' (doc 14) and by killing 'everything in brown uniforms' (doc 18) and mercilessly butchering them (doc 24). This resulted in an escalation of violence, the consequence being 'that hecatombs of people los[t] their lives' (doc 16) and sometimes 'we gave them no quarter at all' (doc 18).

Long-established military traditions, including respect for the enemy on the battlefield, were abandoned as early as the beginning of the campaign and, as an attitude, possibly even before the war had started. Many other texts confirm that Red Army soldiers acted with brutality, which was in turn used by the German army as an excuse to ignore traditional rules of fair combat. And Heinrici, as a general in charge, was well aware of this reaction among his soldiers and neither criticized it nor took action against it. The German–Soviet war was considered an unprecedented conflict and was conducted accordingly. Combatants consequently lost their traditionally accepted status. The devastating fate of Soviet prisoners of war – the suffering of thousands and thousands of men who starved or froze to death, died of diseases or were shot dead during transport, or were 'selected' by Security Police (*Sicherheitspolizei*) and Security Service (*Sicherheitsdienst*) – is one of the darkest chapters of this war.[11] All this was no secret to Heinrici as a senior general, even though it was not his immediate responsibility. In his letters and diaries Heinrici did not discuss the treatment of prisoners of war in great detail. It is fair to assume that someone who thought that no mercy should be shown on the battlefield would not care much about the fate of prisoners. It was not until March 1942, after Heinrici had visited a prison camp, that he criticized the camp conditions and gave orders that they should be improved (doc 120).

Heinrici's rhetoric about 'devious' Red Army soldiers who attacked from ambushes gradually changed over time. He recognized some of the qualities in the Russian soldier: tough and fierce in defence, 'he is a much better soldier than the Frenchman' (doc 15) and, in attack, they are 'like wild animals' (doc 108). His writings show that he had completely underestimated the Red Army in terms of force levels and equipment. Heinrici was particularly impressed that the Red Army relentlessly fought back and inflicted heavy losses on the Wehrmacht despite its own losses and defeats. For him one reason for this resistance was the Russian patriotism that had been triggered by the German attack (doc 33). More importantly, he thought the efficiency of the Bolshevik system of terror was 'defending itself like an angry, disgusting beast' and using all resources in this struggle for existence (doc 27): 'A tremendous energy ruthlessly mobilizes all their forces now and deploys them without mercy.'

It is noticeable in Heinrici's letters that he was almost frightened by the power of Bolshevik ideology and he considered the war as a battle of annihilation between two contrasting *Weltanschauungen* (ideologies). Again and again he identified the 'commissar' as the spine of the resistance and the main representative of the enemy ideology. After the war Heinrici was among those generals who claimed they had strongly opposed the 'commissar order' (*Kommissar-Befehl*) issued on 6 June 1941 and did their best to ensure that it was not put into practice.[12] Different interpretations can be put on his comments about the liquidation of a commissar (doc 72) or a female communist (doc 19), but the underlying tone of his writing does not indicate that he had strong reservations about the order.

Heinrici recognized the unexpected combat strength of the Red Army and the ideological drive of Bolshevism as much as he was impressed by the fanaticism of the partisans. From mid-July 1941 his troops had been confronted with 'miserable guerrilla warfare (*Bandenkrieg*)' (doc 22) and fought a continuous battle 'against this pest' (doc 70), a battle which seemed to be lost from the outset due to the vast, difficult terrain. Heinrici witnessed the fight against the partisans at close quarters – his interpreter shot or lynched several men and women. Time and again Heinrici came across evidence of this type of warfare when he travelled across the country: corpses of executed partisans and 'partisan suspects' hanging from gallows, trees and poles. He was impressed by the courage, determination and huge number of these fanatical fighters, all the more so because they were well aware that 'they would be exterminated without mercy' (doc 64). And yet he did not hesitate to take ruthless action against this 'pest' in order to solve the problem and to achieve a deterrent effect.

Ruthlessness – probably no other word is used more frequently in private and official writings of Wehrmacht generals to characterize the German–Soviet war, and perhaps there is no better word for it. Scenes of horror permeated Heinrici's letters: ruthlessly and without mercy the enemy threw all his forces into battle, leaving a wake of devastation behind him, and he killed from ambushes. However, equally ruthless was the Wehrmacht's method of warfare, in battle, in exploiting the country and in deploying its own forces. This was 'total war', a concept that had been discussed in military publications more than two decades prior to this campaign,[13] but a type of war that had not been experienced in Poland, France or the Balkans. 'There has never been a campaign like the present one,' Heinrici commented after only a few weeks (doc 24). For him, the bloody and fierce battles, the destruction of the country by the scorched-earth policy of the retreating enemy (doc 18) and the effects of the fighting itself and the fleeing and displaced civilians (doc 41) proved that traditional warfare had turned into a merciless struggle for existence between peoples and ideologies. To some extent he had noticed this development already in the First World War, but in the Second the floodgates were opened. He compared the fighting to that of the Thirty Years War, seeing it in terms of images of heaps of corpses and the gallows, which were depicted in the copper engravings by Jacques Callot (doc 70): 'It is like the Thirty Years War, the same habits and customs. Only those who have power have any rights. I have been involved in war for six and a half years, but I have never experienced anything like this.'

This most revealing passage from Heinrici's writings on the eastern campaign indicates that this senior Wehrmacht general recognized the singularity of the German–Soviet war, yet also tolerated it. Both sides adopted the law of the jungle and the concept of the survival of the fittest and most powerful, and abandoned both international law and the normative standards of 'civilized' and 'decent' warfare that had developed in a painstaking process over centuries. 'The kind of warfare we witness here has nothing to do with a decent battle,' Heinrici wrote in response to the Red Army's destruction of Kiev by wireless detonations (doc 49). However, he himself took part in this kind of warfare even though an undercurrent of unease can be detected in his writings. Like many others, Heinrici felt he had to comply with the necessities of war and, as a senior officer, accepted that terror had to be answered with counter-terror and used as a deterrent. In this make-or-break conflict acts of terror could not be avoided. In the hinterland in particular, a minimum number of troops had to employ violent methods in order to achieve the maximum deterrent effect and ensure efficient exploitation.

Occupation policy was as ruthless as warfare. As early as April 1941 Heinrici wrote to his wife that in the Polish deployment area German troops acted without consideration or respect for civilians. He compared this to ancient times 'when the Romans had conquered a foreign people' (doc 5). After the invasion of the Soviet Union German senior commanders were granted extensive responsibilities in the provisional administration and exploitation of the zone in which they operated. Army commanders had executive powers within the area their army occupied and were responsible for the 'security of transportation routes' and the 'exploitation of the country in order to provide for the needs of the troops and gather supplies'.[14] Within the combat zone, commanding generals (of army corps) had to report to army commanders and were obliged to act according to their orders. The notorious so-called *Kriegsgerichtsbarkeitserlass*, issued on 13 May 1941, gave the occupying forces arbitrary and unlimited power to impose their will with brutal force on local people if they showed signs of resistance.

Important orders and decrees from Berlin ignored the tradition that military occupation authorities and generals were obliged to care for the civilians in their area. Commanders in the eastern territories were granted broad freedom of action and could choose to use their power in one way or another. During the first months it was Heinrici's view that the occupation should meet the requirements and needs of the troops. Accordingly, the economic exploitation of the country was more important to him than the fate of the civilians, in the same way as it had been when he was deployed to Romania in 1917. On the second day of the campaign he mocked the theft of horses by the Wehrmacht by calling it the 'liberation' of the population (doc 14). Already at the beginning of July he believed that due to the constant requisitions of food 'the country will be sucked dry soon' (doc 16). Yet he also hoped – and this was a fundamental objective of the campaign – 'to get a lot out of the conquered territories during the next season' (doc 36). During the winter the army's need for supplies from the occupied territories dramatically increased. Since supplies from Germany were inadequate, Heinrici's units had to provision themselves almost entirely from the area they had conquered (doc 88). Like a plague of locusts they infested the country and took the limited food reserves, leaving a state of devastation everywhere (doc 70): 'Soon the region where we are stationed will be completely emptied.'

It was obvious that the ruthless requisitions would have devastating consequences. With reference not only to the widespread destruction but also to the 'emptying' of the country, Heinrici wrote (doc 41): 'Only by considering the details and individual cases can one conceive the destructive power of the war. Probably there will be books written about that matter in the years to come.' Yet Heinrici's writings do not indicate that he was willing to introduce a positive occupation policy giving civilians the chance to survive and hope for the future. To be sure, Heinrici considered that the Soviet people were victims of Bolshevism and recognized that some of them hoped to be 'liberated' by the Germans, and he saw that the Germans had made 'many mistakes' in this context (doc 21). However, he did not draw the obvious conclusions from these reflections.

Instead Heinrici adopted the image of the 'completely passive Russian' who was unable to exploit his own country, which was so rich in resources. Consequently he had to be forced to do so (doc 56). Heinrici described the impact of this alleged attitude and of Bolshevist rule on the country using the same selection of adjectives: depraved, neglected, gloomy, dirty, bleak, primitive. He saw all his anti-Bolshevik and anti-Slav prejudices confirmed by encountering the 'blessings of Bolshevik culture' (doc 21), the 'horrendous state of dilapidation, depredation and dirt caused by Bolshevism' (doc 41) and the basically good-natured Russian, cruel in battle but without initiative in everyday life, with whom it was 'impossible to make any progress' (doc 82). This experience of conditions in the Soviet Union seemed to justify ignoring the conventions of war during the campaign. Disregarding the fate of millions of civilians for ideological and utilitarian reasons resulted in breaches of traditional and 'decent' ways of warfare. This is clearly true for Heinrici, but not only for him. In October 1941, when it seemed that Moscow was about to be captured, he wrote (doc 57): 'We might go into this nest of communists or let them all starve and freeze to death instead of bothering with exhausting street fights. We'll see about that!'

When on 30 March 1941 Hitler demanded that the generals had to 'overcome their reservations in this war of annihilation',[15] Heinrici complied without even having heard the speech. The long-established ideal of a 'clean' war related to 'chivalrous' behaviour towards military opponents and the 'decent' treatment of civilians. The military elite brushed aside these traditional standards, which were not important in the merciless struggle against the Red Army and the ruthless exploitation of the occupied territories. The generals accepted and stuck to Hitler's rules of a war of conquest and ideology. Heinrici, who was well capable of reflection, was neither ignorant nor unduly submissive in doing so; he was fully aware of Hitler's war aims and their consequences. The new military doctrine of 'total war', the cruelty and ruthlessness of the Bolshevik arch-enemy and the deplorable state of the Soviet Union and its people, which was considered far below western standards, served as excuses for his conduct.

In a very distinctive passage in one of his letters Heinrici described how strange and foreign this country seemed to him (doc 56): 'These people cannot be judged by our standards. I believe it would be better and more appropriate to approach this country not gradually by foot as we do, but by ship leaving the home shores, breaking away from everything we are familiar with and discovering it like a foreign, unknown continent.' Apparently Heinrici felt like a modern conquistador stepping onto an unexplored continent and leaving the norms of western Christianity far behind. This seemed to justify the rupture in civilized behaviour: was the German army not forced to disregard the standards of civilization in an environment as uncivilized as this? In these circumstances Heinrici's values deteriorated, even though he was a conservative Christian officer. The episode of the 'dead Russian' (doc 73) illustrates this: for several weeks Heinrici used the unburied body of a fallen enemy as a landmark and turning point of his walks.

Heinrici's attitude towards Jews was also marked by a decline in values. This was already obvious before the invasion of the Soviet Union when he was still in the General Government of Poland. The 'awful Jews wearing the star of David on their sleeves' annoyed

Heinrici just as much as the 'bugs' and 'lice' which he mentioned in the same sentence (doc 4). Coldly, without indignation, he described the enslavement of the Jewish (and Polish) population, their starvation which was instigated and tolerated by German authorities, their impoverishment and ghettoization. Thus he was fully aware of the Nazi policy towards the Jews in occupied Poland. Yet he failed to fundamentally oppose the regime in the same way he had failed to oppose it when he witnessed the first anti-Semitic steps taken in the Reich.

The appalling conditions in the General Government were a foretaste of the campaign against the Soviet Union, which proved to be radically different from the war in France, mainly because of the ruthlessness of the German army. After his experiences in Poland, it is unlikely that Heinrici was even slightly surprised by the brutal treatment of Slavs and Jews in the conquered Soviet territories. His private writings do not reveal whether he knew about the mass murders committed by the *SS-Einsatzgruppen*, or what he thought about them.[16] However, the anti-Semitic concept of 'Jewish Bolshevism' appears rather indirectly in a letter to his wife, in which he described the 'blessings of Bolshevik culture', adding: 'Walls and ceilings are covered with painted Stars of David' (doc 21). Heinrici's anti-Semitism is unmistakable, and it is fair to assume that he was not concerned about the fate of the Jewish population, even though he might not have agreed to their mass murder.

This is where the limitations of Heinrici's writings become most obvious. While they are extremely revealing in terms of his views on the German–Soviet war and its special character, they do not say much about Heinrici's actions. Yet the conduct of the Wehrmacht's generals was determined by their perceptions and their image of the war. Heinrici's writings also shed light on his view of the special character of the war in the east which led him to disregard the consequences of a policy of 'total war' waged between peoples and ideologies. Given Heinrici's responsibility as a senior commander, this was a highly questionable attitude.

General Heinrici showed an almost fatherly sense of responsibility towards his soldiers and a huge commitment to them, and in this respect he was certainly an exemplary leader. The same man, however, was completely passive, even indifferent, towards the obvious crimes committed in this war, which he was clearly aware of. And, even though he agreed with several political objectives and policies of the Nazi regime, he was not a fanatical National Socialist. This raises the question of whether the actions of the Wehrmacht generals during the war against the Soviet Union can be sufficiently explained by reference to National Socialism.

Comparing Heinrici's attitudes, as analysed in the last chapter, with his perception of the war during the first year of the eastern campaign sheds some light on this issue. Commonly held anti-Bolshevik feelings among the traditional elite, combined with anti-Slav and anti-Jewish sentiments and the increasingly radical military doctrine of the inter-war period, formed an explosive mixture that could easily be ignited by the National Socialists.

This attitude, developed and deepened in the aftermath of the First World War, explains why Heinrici as a senior officer tolerated – and accepted – the brutalization of warfare that made the eastern campaign different from others. This viewpoint was not National Socialist as such, although Nazi ideology obviously shaped and enhanced it. Furthermore, the totalitarian state was very attractive for a nationalist and conservative officer like Heinrici as he saw many aspects of modern military policy, authoritarian domestic policy and expansive foreign policy pursued by the Nazi regime. It seemed as if the old hegemonic dreams of the Wilhelmine period might come true at last. It is no surprise that the military still thought in imperial and colonial terms during the first stage of the eastern campaign. The prospect of a conquest in the east was so attractive that the ugly side of the dictatorship was disregarded.

Heinrici's scepticism, which later turned into criticism, was not directed against these political aims but against the way in which they were put into practice – not against the regime as such but against the tactics that were adopted and the operational details. It is fair to assume that many of the insights that come from an analysis of Heinrici's private writings are also true for most of the other senior generals on the Eastern Front. In his political thinking, Heinrici was a typical member of the national conservative military elite who served Hitler and the Nazi Dictatorship from beginning to end.

Chapter 5

Outlook

When it became apparent in the winter of 1941/42 that the blitzkrieg against the Soviet Union had failed, the Wehrmacht generals were deeply shocked. They now had to prepare themselves for a long-lasting war which would demand different military tactics and occupation policies than those planned for a campaign of only a few months. Yet despite the uncertain prospect, Heinrici took a more optimistic view of the overall situation after the Soviet counteroffensive came to an end in May 1942. At the beginning of November 1942 he still described the German situation as 'satisfactory'[1] and was pleased with 'a very confident speech of the Fuehrer'.[2]

It was not until the Allied landings in North Africa and the encirclement and subsequent annihilation of the 6th Army at Stalingrad that Heinrici's comments became more pessimistic. He increasingly recognized the 'adding [of] a new uber-strong enemy' in the east (doc 3, FN) and noted that 'those responsible assessed Russia incorrectly'.[3] Heinrici also disapproved of senior Wehrmacht figures who were not standing up to Hitler.[4] With regard to the operational and tactical aspects of the war, and from his perspective as a defence expert, he primarily criticized them for 'holding an opinion that looked bold and brave and favoured the tactics of persevering instead of admitting that surrender or retreat would be more sensible. And yet carrying out short-term defensive manoeuvres would have gained double success.'[5] After the defeat at Stalingrad Heinrici drew a sobering conclusion:[6] 'All in all, the German Army has overreached itself. It faced problems which could only be avoided if the enemy – like France – completely collapsed. When he didn't – like in the east – the leaders lacked sense and wisdom.'

Obviously, this criticism was also directed against Hitler. In September 1943 Heinrici predicted imminent defeat and for the first time expressed reservations about the Nazi regime:[7] 'What was once regarded by the people as an object of admiration and idolatry is collapsing.' Yet these views did not lead him to oppose the regime fundamentally, let alone to play a role other than that of the obedient army commander. Instead he reacted in the same way as the German population in July 1943:[8] They were all 'willing to endure, because everybody is aware that in this war defeat is not an option, since whatever would come after it is simply unthinkable.' Opposition and resistance or even mutiny and *coup d'état* were not compatible with the concept of a battle for existence. For the time being Heinrici put aside his uneasiness about the dictatorship, which had been growing since 1942. He opposed the assassination plot of 20 July 1944,[9] although afterwards he put in a good word – albeit without success – for Schulze-Büttger, one of the plotters he was acquainted with.[10]

Even during the dramatic last weeks of the war Heinrici was not willing to take action to bring an early end to the dictatorship and the fighting. When, in mid-April 1945 Albert Speer approached him with plans to assassinate Hitler in view of the 'Nero Decree' (Hitler's order to destroy the German infrastructure so that it could not be of any use to the Allies), Heinrici claimed to have answered:[11] 'At worst I can imagine refusing to obey, which is linked to my oath. But as a soldier I cannot murder the supreme commander to whom I have sworn allegiance, even less in face of the attacking enemy!' Two weeks later he clashed with Keitel and Jodl, because he feared their orders would cause needless casualties, which he could not reconcile with his conscience. Yet instead of being insubordinate and acting on his own authority, he resigned from his post. 'They told me to eliminate these people, take them prisoners or do what you like. If I had done so the German people would have seen in me the man, the soldier, who betrayed the Fuehrer at the last moment. They would have said: If it was not for this traitor, everything could have gone the other way.'[12]

Early signs of the defeat in the east, such as the crisis at Moscow, increased Heinrici's misgivings but did not change his attitude towards the Nazi regime. Up to the bitter end he served Hitler as an obedient soldier. In his zone of command he concluded that since the Soviet Union, unlike France, did not collapse after the initial military setbacks, it was much stronger and more resistant than expected. After the winter crisis had been overcome, and when he returned to the Eastern Front in July 1942, he again took an interest in Russian civilians. During the quiet period in the central sector of the front from mid-1942 to mid-1943, he had a much better opportunity to study the country and its people than he had done during the period of mobile warfare and defensive battles. As an army commander he had to oversee the occupation policy in his part of the front, and the situation did not change there for several months.

As early as August 1942 Heinrici 'got a completely different impression of the people here', who used to be considered 'merely as partisans' by the Wehrmacht.[13] From now on he made efforts to establish an occupation policy that was – at least to some extent – constructive in order to encourage the population to cooperate and to minimize the threat represented by partisans. When a skilfully staged harvest festival in 1942 was successful – 'a psychological victory with regard to the control of the Russian people' – Heinrici hoped that the mood of the local people would change in favour of the German occupiers.[14] He was now of the opinion that Russia 'has to be conquered not against but with the Russians'. He thought it would be easy to manipulate this 'sentimental people' by 'being responsive and supportive'.[15] Despite some reservations,[16] he persevered with this approach and in early 1943 he was pleased to state that, in the area controlled by the 4th Army, 'the Russian people are more cooperative because they are treated decently'[17] than in any other sector.

'Necessities of war', however, hindered his efforts to establish a 'decent' and positive occupation policy from the outset. Firstly, the food situation for the population remained very tense. The Wehrmacht, which was partly responsible for the shortages, was not able to improve the 'miserable lives' of the local people, in particular those of the children.[18] Secondly, the forced recruitment of Russian labourers, who had to till the fields and dig trenches in the Soviet Union or to work in the German Reich, had disastrous consequences for Russian families. In contrast to his sentiments during the early stage of the campaign, Heinrici's comments on this situation showed some compassion and pity:[19] 'One has to feel sorry for the native population. Everything here is a mess.'

Yet Heinrici could not prevent the exploitation of civilians for military reasons. In particular the withdrawal of his army group in March 1943 caused unbearable hardships for the Russian population as several villages were burnt down and many civilians who were fit for work were deported.[20] This reckless policy, carried out in the name of 'total war', counteracted the positive efforts that had been made. In Heinrici's opinion, the civilians in the occupied territories formed three groups:[21] first, the growing partisan movement and their supporters; second, the anti-Bolsheviks who cooperated with the Germans; and, third, people who favoured neither side but were scared of both.

Thus it was the campaign that failed first, followed by the occupation rule and finally by the entire war.

The problems of occupation politics confirmed Heinrici's perception of Russia as a strange and foreign country, 'an alien, backward culture, not belonging to our Europe, but to a different continent'.[22] However, compared with his negative feelings about the country during the first months of the campaign, he now gained something positive out of the experience. He was deeply impressed by 'the primeval, the elemental, that shapes everything in this huge country. The countryside is still unspoilt. Here nature prevails unbridled. Here only the healthy and strong survive against its attacks.'[23] His belief in the superior toughness of the Soviet soldier – which did not fit in the National Socialist concept of the inferiority of Slav peoples – was based on the social Darwinism of this analysis.[24] The longer the war lasted, the greater became Heinrici's respect for the 'uber-strong enemy' (doc 3, FN). Fighting the Russians was no longer about realizing imperialistic aims but was a simple struggle to survive. More than ever this served as an excuse for the fierce and ruthless defensive war waged by the Wehrmacht. Heinrici accepted, and agreed with, the order to annihilate the enemy without mercy, especially the partisans.[25]

However, from now on he had second thoughts about German 'total' warfare. He was not unmoved when the Soviet government denounced him and Model as war criminals.[26] It became clear to him that the degree of ruthlessness might be controlled in a short campaign, but all inhibitions would be forgotten during a longer conflict. The withdrawal of Army Group Centre from its positions during the spring of 1943 caused a level of devastation which in his opinion exceeded the necessities of war. He could not bear the 'constant burning and destroying'[27] and tried to take measures against the aimless, uncontrolled implementation of the 'scorched-earth strategy', for instance, in September when his army group withdrew from Smolensk.[28]

The brutalization of warfare reached a point where 'every baggage commander feels called upon to destroy something'.[29] Heinrici repudiated this development, referring back to his military training and a different military tradition,[30] yet he realized that the process was irreversible.[31] 'The war here has reached a state which exceeds the Thirty Years War by far. All my attempts to stop these incidents, which I abhor, have been futile, and left me feeling powerless. The practice of soldiering in this campaign lacks satisfaction.' And in March 1944 he summarized:[32] 'As soon as one outbreak had been dealt with, another one occurred elsewhere. It was a disease spreading all over the place; one could not fight it in spite of all orders and counter-measures.'

However, this 'disease' was a consequence of the type of warfare that stemmed from Hitler's political and ideological ideas, which the Wehrmacht had accepted knowingly and deliberately in June 1941. Just like the sorcerer's apprentice in Goethe's poem, the spirits roused by Wehrmacht leaders and accepted by front commanders now ignored their commands. The military thought that they could control and benefit from these ruthless methods during the mobile campaign of Operation Barbarossa. Yet after the initially successful campaign failed, the moral degeneration that occurred during the months of uncontrolled warfare and unauthorized occupation turned out to be too profound to be reversed by disciplinary measures. Later the generals justified themselves by referring to their attempts to maintain order and discipline and to their revised approach to the occupation policy. This apologetic defence, however, is less than convincing. The significance of the first year – and particularly its first half – of the German–Soviet war can hardly be overestimated, because it pointed the way to the brutality that followed and had momentous consequences. Heinrici's writings are the direct and blunt testimony of a senior general with good observational skills and an interest in many aspects of the war beyond purely military questions. That is what makes them especially valuable.

Chapter 6

Notes to Part I

Chapter 1: Introduction

1. Gotthard Heinrici's estate is located in Bundesarchiv-Militärarchiv Freiburg (henceforth: BA-MA) and comprises 161 volumes with documents from his entire life and service time.
2. Apart from popular scientific accounts based on documentary reports about the Battle of Berlin in March/April 1945. Here Heinrici plays a major role and is characterized as a prudent, able but apolitical general. See mainly Ryan: *Kampf*, who refers to conversations with Heinrici and to documents provided by him.
3. However, the diaries of two commanders of army groups have been published: Leeb: *Tagebuchaufzeichnungen*; Bock: *Pflicht*. At army command level there are only a few letters of the 1st General Staff officer of the 4th Army available (October 1941–October 1942); Stieff: *Briefe*, pp. 129–58. The published records of the escort officer of the commanding general of the LIII Army Corps, a unit which was positioned close to Heinrici's troops for a short period, give an insight into General Weisenberger's leadership and the course of the battle rather than into his mentality: *'Fahrtberichte' aus der Zeit des deutsch-sowjetischen Krieges*.
4. *See* the letter to his wife, 24 January 1942, in: BA-MA, N 265/156, fol. 16: 'Keep all these pages in a safe place. They are documents.'
5. *See* Hürter: *Hitlers Heerführer*.

Chapter 2: Life and Career

1. Dates and facts according to Heinrici's personal file: BA-MA, Pers 6/30. Brief biographical notes can be found in Möller-Witten: 'Heinrici'; Philippi: 'Heinrici'; Brausch and Hubatsch: 'Heinrici'.
2. For the military course of the campaign against the Soviet Union from the German onslaught to the winter crisis in February

1942, *see Das Deutsche Reich und der Zweite Weltkrieg* (henceforth: *DRZW*), vol. 4, pp. 451–652 (article Ernst Klink). *See also* Reinhardt: *Wende;* Hartmann: *Wehrmacht;* Glantz: *Operation Barbarossa;* Stahel: *Operation Barbarossa;* Stahel: *Battle;* Stahel: *March.*

Chapter 3: Heinrici's Character

1. *See* Hürter: *Hitlers Heerführer. See also* Messerschmidt: *Wehrmacht;* Müller: *Heer;* Müller: 'Armee. Versuch'; Kroener: 'Veränderungen'.
2. Heinrici's memoirs, 'Der Krieg', 1960, in: BA-MA, N 265/23, fol. 6.
3. Heinrici's memoirs on his schooldays, 1960, in: BA-MA, N 265/24, fos. 26f.
4. Ibid, fos. 20 and 27. *See also* ibid., fol. 20: 'It was certainly not a piece of art, yet it anticipated incidents which we had to face half a century later.'
5. In his First World War memoirs from 1960, Heinrici emphasizes that he was 'completely occupied with my personal experiences which have vividly remained in my mind until today.' In: BA-MA, N 265/23, fol. 1.
6. Ibid., fol. 2. These impressions also dominate his further recollections of this period. 'Meine dienstliche Verwendung im 1. Weltkrieg', c. 1960, ibid., fos. 57f.; 'Wiedersehen mit Gumbinnen', 1960, in: BA-MA, N 265/24, fos. 42–5. *See also* ibid., fol. 44: 'It is said that some owners were even murdered or abducted. In any case, the occupation of the enemy had left its mark which demonstrated how fundamentally different their views and beliefs were from ours.' In hindsight, Heinrici also believed ('Der Krieg', in: BA-MA, N 265/23, fol. 3) that: 'The Russians of the First World War were tame guys compared to their Bolshevist descendants in the Second World War.'
7. 'Meine dienstliche Verwendung im 1. Weltkrieg', c. 1960, in: BA-MA, N 265/23, fol. 59.
8. *See* ibid., fol. 61, on the deployment in October 1914: 'We arrived at the banks of the River Vistula and found that there was only sand, panje huts full of lice, storm and rain.'
9. Heinrici's diary entry, 22 February 1917, in: BA-MA, N 265/8.
10. For the encounter with the 'industrial technological war', *see* Müller: 'Armee. Versuch.' *See also* the still fundamental studies

of Michael Geyer, in particular: *Aufrüstung*. Although Geyer exaggerated his sometimes anachronistic argument, his terms 'industrialisation', 'delimitation (*Entgrenzung*)' and 'societalisation (*Vergesellschaftung*)' of war aptly describe the intensive discussion on military theory in the interwar period, summarized in the phrase 'total war'. *See also* Förster: *Krieg*; Bitzel: *Konzeption*. For an interesting approach to the influence of these experiences and conclusions on the campaign against the Soviet Union, *see* Friedrich: *Gesetz*, passim.

11. Type of war in Europe during the period of absolute monarchies involving small armies and limited goals.
12. Heinrici's diary entry, 15 October 1918, in: BA-MA, N 265/8: 'We can expect a proper mess in Germany after the war. I assume that things will happen along the lines of Russia.'
13. Heinrici's diary entry, 16 October 1918, ibid.
14. Heinrici's memoirs, 'Der Krieg', 1960, in: BA-MA, N 265/23, fol. 22. On signs of dissolution in the army, *see* ibid., fos. 22–6.
15. *See* Heinrici, 'Die Jahre nach dem 1. Weltkrieg in Königsberg', c. 1960, in: BA-MA, N 265/31, fos. 1–20, quote: fol. 1.
16. *See also* Heinrici's diary entry, 27 June 1919, in: BA-MA, N 265/8, blaming the government for '[being] responsible for dropping us'. 'It was their damned duty to refuse or if signing to let us deal with things tacitly.'
17. Literally 'people's community', a term that originally became popular during the First World War and was adopted by the Nazis.
18. Heinrici's diary entry, 17 October 1918, in: BA-MA, N 265/8: 'If the demands of all the corrupt peoples such as the Poles, Czechs, Hungarians or whatever they are called are going to be realized, then we will enter an era of war and revolution more than ever.'
19. *See* Heinrici's curriculum vitae compiled by himself, in: BA-MA, N 265/26, fol. 17.
20. Heinrici to his parents, Osterode/Ostpreußen, 5 March 1932, in: BA-MA, N 265/147, fos. 72f.
21. Heinrici to his mother, Osterode/Ostpreußen, 19 March 1932, ibid., fos. 76f.
22. Heinrici to his parents, Berlin, 4 February 1933, in: BA-MA, N 265/148, fol. 11.

23. Heinrici to his parents, Berlin, 17 February 1933, ibid., fos. 16f. See also ibid.: 'Meanwhile the government has taken drastic measures. Among civil servants it has cleaned up. To ban the Berlin based newspapers (asphalt press) dragging everything through the mud was something after my own heart. ... They also find the right tone now in Geneva ...'
24. Heinrici to his parents, Berlin, 24 February 1933, ibid., fos. 19f.
25. Heinrici to his father, Berlin, 10 March 1933, ibid., fos. 28–30. *See also* the letters to his parents from 4 March 1933 (ibid., fol. 24), 20 March 1933 (ibid., fos. 34f.), 1 April 1933 (ibid., fol. 37), 9 April 1933 (ibid., fol. 39), 20 July 1933 (ibid., fos. 70f.), 6 August 1933 (ibid., fos. 77–9).
26. Heinrici to his parents, Berlin, 1 April 1933, ibid., fol. 37.
27. Ibid.
28. Heinrici to his parents, Berlin, 20 July 1933, ibid., fos. 70f.
29. Heinrici to his parents, Berlin, 4 March 1933, ibid., fol. 24.
30. *See also* the letters to his parents, 4 March 1933 (ibid., fol. 24), 20 March 1933 (ibid., fos. 34f.) and 11 November 1933 (ibid., fos. 99f.)
31. Heinrici to his parents, Berlin, 2 June 1933, ibid., fol. 57.
32. Heinrici to his parents, Berlin, 20 March 1933, ibid., fos. 34f.
33. Ibid.
34. Heinrici to his parents, Berlin, 1 April 1933, ibid., fol. 37.
35. Heinrici to his parents, Berlin, 9 April 1933, ibid., fol. 39.
36. Heinrici to his parents, Berlin, 6 August 1933, ibid., fos. 77–9. *See also* ibid.: 'In doing so, the escaped Jews do a disservice to the decent ones.'
37. Heinrici to his mother, 18 November 1938, in: BA-MA, N 265/152, fol. 85: 'In Berlin and in all other cities Jewish shops and synagogues are destroyed. ... Everywhere people are condemning what has happened.'
38. Detmold, city in Northrhine-Westphalia, in 1939 capital of the Free state of Lippe.
39. Alfred Rosenberg was leader of the foreign policy office of the NSDAP and one of the main authors of Nazi ideology.
40. Heinrici to his mother, 16 January 1939, in: BA-MA, N 265/153, fos. 6f.
41. See his retrospective account in a letter to Foertsch dated 28 June 1951, in: Institut für Zeitgeschichte, Munich (henceforth: IfZ), ZS 66/2: 'I fully supported the national spirit of the NSDAP, its

fight for equal rights of the German people and the army. First and foremost I appreciated the intention to reintegrate the workers into the state for whose sake I accepted things in its social agenda which I thought went too far.' He claimed to have had reservations about the radical racism and the revolutionary attitude of the party.

42. Heinrici to his parents, Berlin, 7 July 1934, in: BA-MA, N 265/149, fos. 36–9.
43. In this context Heinrici had a first extended meeting with Hitler in December 1934. See the letter to his parents, 29 December 1934, ibid., fos. 74–6. The soldiers' leagues were founded in December 1935 without gaining much importance.
44. From Heinrici's speech at the flag consecration of the Labour Front (*Arbeitsfront*) in Münster, 1938, in: BA-MA, N 265/33, fos. 9–20: 'The flags of the Wehrmacht and the Labour Front look different at first sight. As different as the tasks of a soldier and a worker are. Yet both flags have one thing in common: the swastika. It is the sign of the *Weltanschauung* they have both in common. This very *Weltanschauung* was missing in 1918, and that was the reason for the downfall of the second Empire.' Heinrici, addressing recruits in Münster on 27 February 1938, ibid, fos. 26f.: 'The principles of the old army enabled our people to defy a world of enemies for four years. It is these principles we, the new Wehrmacht, want to convey to you. These principles will give you an understanding of the National Socialist *Weltanschauung* born from the spirit of soldiership.'
45. *See also* his positive impressions of the Nuremberg Rally in 1937: Heinrici to his parents, Berlin, 10 September 1937, in: BA-MA, N 265/151, fos. 106f.
46. Heinrici's remarks on a speech by Himmler show his thoughts about the 'policy of internal order' ('*Ordnungspolitik*'): 'His lecture on the concentration camps he is responsible for was rather interesting. I can imagine that they have mustered some awful people there.' Heinrici to his parents, Berlin, 19 January 1937, in: BA-MA, N 265/151, fol. 6.
47. Heinrici to his mother, Münster, 13 February 1938, in: BA-MA, N 265/152, fos. 11f.
48. Heinrici to his parents, Berlin, 7 July 1933, in: BA-MA, N 265/148, fol. 67.

49. Heinrici's diary entry from 29 September 1938, in: BA-MA, N 265/9.
50. *See*, for instance, his letter to his wife during the Sudeten crisis, Münster, 19 September 1938, in: BA-MA, N 265/154, fol. 34.
51. *See* Müller: *Heer*, pp. 255–377.
52. Hitler's speech addressing high-ranking commanders of the Wehrmacht on 25 January 1939 in the Reichskanzlei, in: Müller: *Armee. Darstellung*, pp. 360–5. Heinrici was not present when Hitler spoke to troop commanders in the Kroll opera on 10 February 1939 (ibid., pp. 365–75). Heinrici's transcript of the speech from 25 January, in: BA-MA, N 265/9.
53. *Lebensraum*, literally living space, was a key term in Nazi ideology and expansionism. The Nazis claimed that Germany was overpopulated due to the new borders established in the Versailles Treaty and that therefore the German people had the right to expand to the east.
54. Address by Heinrici, 20 April 1939, in: BA-MA, N 265/33, fol. 46. *See also* ibid.: 'We are right in the middle of the development. It is not over yet. It is in these very days that we witness how the world unites against us to challenge the Fuehrer and the German people for its victories. We know that they will fail if the German people are devoted and united in following the Fuehrer.'
55. Heinrici's diary entry, 1 September 1939, in: BA-MA, N 265/9.
56. Heinrici's diary entry, late September 1939, ibid.
57. Heinrici's diary entry, 16 April 1940, ibid.
58. Heinrici's diary entry, 24 June 1940, in: BA-MA, N 265/10.
59. Ibid.
60. Heinrici's diary entry, 12 September 1940, in: BA-MA, N 265/9. 'I have suggested to Sodenstern to move our corps headquarters later on to England as needed – even in contrast to preliminary plans. The prospect of staying here as an occupation army is neither glorious nor honourable. ... I have been in combat for merely two days, this is the only time that I could prove myself as a leader.'
61. Heinrici's diary entry, 29 January 1941, in: BA-MA, N 265/10, fos. 56f.: 'Both in the Mediterranean and around the British Isles it becomes clear that we fight for international standing [*Weltgeltung*] and have no navy.'

62. Heinrici's diary entry, 22 November 1940, ibid., fos. 27f. The Soviet Union was supposed to be won over by offering compensation in Central Asia and by opening the Dardanelles.
63. Heinrici's diary entry, 29 August 1939, in: BA-MA, N 265/9: 'An alliance with Russia is certainly in the interest of the German people.'
64. Heinrici's diary entry, 13 September 1939, ibid.

Chapter 4: War Images

1. Stenographic proceedings of Heinrici's examination on 15 October 1947, in: IfZ, MA 1569, roll 26.
2. *See* Müller-Hillebrandt: *Heer*, vol. 1, pp. 84–92. *See also Heeresdruckvorschrift (H.Dv.g 92): Handbuch für den Generalstabsdienst im Kriege*, part 1, Berlin 1939.
3. The following definitions are based on Frieser: *Blitzkrieg-Legende*, pp. 7f.
4. On 18 December 1941 Hitler ordered in his so called *Haltebefehl* the front to be defended 'fanatically' and forbade any withdrawal. *See* Hürter: *Hitlers Heerführer*, pp. 326f.
5. The interesting discussion on the 'deprofessionalization' of the officer corps (*see* for example Wegner: *Defensive*; Petter: *Massengesellschaft*) hardly applies to Heinrici. Since warfare strategy was not part of his responsibilities and he was only to a certain extent involved in large-scale operational planning, he did not have the opportunity to fail, as Wegner argues, correctly claiming that the officer corps proved themselves incompetent to react with an adequate strategy to the looming defeat. However, Heinrici excelled in all aspects of tactical command.
6. Literally 'tub track'. The Kübelwagen was a light military vehicle produced by Volkswagenwerk GmbH.
7. The Fieseler Storch, literally Fieseler's Stork, was a very light liaison aircraft.
8. In September 1941 Heinrici was awarded the Knight's Cross, because on 11 August 1941 he had crossed the River Dnieper in a rubber boat at the head of his troops. *See* Thomas: *Eichenlaub-Träger*, vol. 1, p. 263.
9. *See also On the German Art of War. Truppenführung*, ed. Bruce Condell and David T. Zabecki (Boulder: Lynne Rienner Publishers, 2001; German original: *Heeresdruckvorschrift (H.Dv. 300/1): Truppenführung*, part 1, Berlin 1936): 'The personal

influence of the commander on his troops is vitally important. He must position himself close to the combat units' (p. 36). 'During pursuit operations the commander must move with the forward elements. His presence in the front line will inspire his units' (p. 38).

10. For the negative image of Russia held by the German military elite during the German–Soviet war, *see* Förster: *Rußlandbild.*
11. *See* Streit: *Keine Kameraden*; Streim: *Behandlung.*
12. Stenographic proceedings of Heinrici's examination on 15 October 1947, in: IfZ, MA 1569, roll 26. On 9 July 1941 the XXXXIII Army Corps reported to the 2nd Army it had shot dead four 'commissars' up to 5 July 1941; *see* IfZ, MA 1564, roll 29, NOKW-2263. In the corps' files (BA-MA, RH 24–43) there is no documentation on the Ic department and the department of the quartermaster from April 1941 to March 1943. The question of how 'commissars', prisoners of war, partisans, Jews and civilians in Heinrici's area of command were treated has to be reconstructed based on other sources. *See also* Römer: *Kommissarbefehl*, p. 607.
13. *See* for example Adalbert von Taysen: Krieg, in: *Handbuch der neuzeitlichen Wehrwissenschaften*, vol. I, pp. 171–5. This official manual served as a reference book for every officer. *See* p. 173: 'War turns into total war and bears its original features again, features of the war of all against all.' In the preface to the *Handbuch* Minister of War Blomberg wrote: 'Only a genuine understanding of the nature of the war of the present time can unleash the nation's power which is required to prevail its nationhood (*Volkstum*) and its lebensraum in the long run.'
14. Order of the Commander-in-Chief of the Army (*Besondere Anordnungen für die Versorgung*, attachment 6, part C), 3 April 1941, in: *Fall Barbarossa*, pp. 299–304, quote: p. 299. *See also DRZW*, vol. 5/1, pp. 80f. (article by Hans Umbreit). It was planned that at a later time the civil administration would take over administration and exploitation of the country for the benefit of the homeland. Yet in many areas this civil administration was never established.
15. Halder: *Kriegstagebuch*, vol. 2, p. 337.
16. During the investigations of the public prosecutor of Hamburg against former members of the Sonderkommando 7b, Heinrici in 1968 denied any knowledge of the massacres (and of

Enterdungsmaßnahmen, exhumation actions to hide any evidence of the killings). *See* documents in: BA-MA, N 265/57.

Chapter 5: Outlook

1. Heinrici's diary entry, 5 November 1942, in: BA-MA, N 265/13: 'Overall result: the war is not yet won. However, there is no reason to be worried. Militarily and in terms of food supplies the situation is satisfactory. Yet there are shortages, e.g. fuel.'
2. Heinrici's diary entry, 8 November 1942, ibid: 'Even better and more impressive than the one at the opening of the *Winterhilfswerk* (winter relief).'
3. Heinrici's diary entry, 22 January 1943, ibid.
4. Heinrici's diary entry, 19 February 1943, ibid. This criticism was primarily directed against Halder and Zeitzler.
5. Ibid: 'This is all psychological. Before and during the war leading figures have often been in opposition to the Fuehrer's military wishes. Colonel-General von Fritsch, Beck, General von Wietersheim were all against his plans. They seemed to be defeatists and they were proven wrong with regard to the problems at the time in question.'
6. Ibid.
7. Heinrici to his wife, 6 September 1943, in: BA-MA, N 265/157, fos. 98–101. See also ibid: 'This is the last stage of the war. We have to be very clear about that. It is no longer in our power to change course. That is over.'
8. Heinrici's diary entry, 5 July 1943, in: BA-MA, N 265/13.
9. *See* Heinrici's letter to his children, 27 July 1944, in: BA-MA, N 265/158, fol. 100: 'We were all completely taken aback by the sad incidents in Germany during the last days. It is a miracle that the explosion did not harm the Fuehrer.'
10. Reinecke (Chief of the OKW NS guidance staff) to Heinrici, Berlin, 24 October 1944, in: BA-MA, N 265/35, fol. 54.
11. Note by Heinrici shortly after the end of the war, in: BA-MA, N 265/114. Speer: *Erinnerungen*, S. 471; according to his report the conversation with Heinrici took place on 15 April 1945. Speer does not mention the subject of this discussion.
12. Heinrici to his wife, Niebüll, 5 May 1945, in: BA-MA, N 265/158, fos. 137–46. 'Your husband, the pessimist, is right in the end. This is the end that I have anticipated a long time ago. God's judgement is gruesome and horrible. And this is just the

beginning. Who knows what serious consequences will still happen. Terrible inner shocks, heartaches, doubts and inner fights I have fought during the last three weeks. Duty, obedience, conscience and my own conviction have battled against each other.'

13. Heinrici to his wife, 16 August 1942, in: BA-MA, N 265/156, fos. 67f.
14. Heinrici's diary entry, 7 October 1942, in: BA-MA, N 265/13. *See also* Heinrici to his wife, 12 October 1942, in: BA-MA, N 265/156, fol. 85.
15. Heinrici's diary entry, 7 October 1942, in: BA-MA, N 265/13.
16. *See* ibid: 'But I think it will be difficult to achieve. Obviously there are a lot of people here who are enemies of Bolshevism and reject the present system in Russia. Yet there are even more who are convinced enemies of Germany and opposed to us regardless.'
17. Heinrici to his family, 30 January 1943, in: BA-MA, N 265/157, fos. 14f.
18. *See* Heinrici to his wife, 30 July 1942, in: BA-MA, N 265/156, fol. 62: 'The people here and particularly the children live in miserable conditions. They are happy about every bit they get from us.'
19. Heinrici to his family, 28 March 1943, in: BA-MA, N 265/157, fol. 31.
20. *See also* ibid: 'So many families are torn apart, one family member remains at home, another is building roads or bunkers, the third has to do farm work in Münster. They do not know where they will be in future, their property and meagre belongings are lost. They are in fact grateful when we give them food. It takes the Russian's ability to suffer and his submissiveness to endure all this.'
21. Heinrici to his family, 16 April 1943, ibid, fos. 74–6.
22. Heinrici's diary entry, 23 November 1942, in: BA-MA, N 265/13.
23. Heinrici to his family, 15 April 1943, in: BA-MA, N 265/157, fol. 74.
24. *See* ibid: 'And this explains why the Russian soldier is superior to his German counterpart in many respects such as in practical things and in his toughness towards nature and its challenges.' *See also* Heinrici to his wife, 30 July 1942, about the survival of scattered soldiers in: BA-MA, N 265/156, fol. 62: 'They are like

animals, our men would never endure and survive a time like this.'

25. Heinrici to his family, 16 April 1943, in: BA-MA, N 265/157, fos. 74–6.
26. Ibid; Heinrici to his wife, 8 April 1943, ibid, fos. 41–3.
27. Heinrici's diary entry, 19 September 1943, in: BA-MA, N 265/43, fol. 125.
28. *See also* BA-MA, N 265/46. Ibid, *see* further orders by Heinrici prohibiting uncontrolled destructions. Even after several months the Luftwaffe still complained about Heinrici's reactions in Smolensk to Hitler, who demanded his response. *See* Busch (Commander-in-Chief of Army Group Centre) to Heinrici, 15 June 1944, in: ibid, fol. 6.
29. Heinrici's diary entry, 18 March 1944, in: BA-MA, N 265/14.
30. Heinrici to his family, 3 November 1943, in: BA-MA, N 265/157, fol. 120: 'Warfare used to be different, it was not just destruction. That is not in me, we have been brought up differently.'
31. Heinrici to his family, 10 October 1943, ibid, fol. 110.
32. Heinrici's diary entry, 18 March 1944, in: BA-MA, N 265/14.

PART II

Documents

Chapter 7

General Heinrici – in his own words

After the armistice with France on 22 June 1940, General Heinrici's XXXXIII Army Corps was relocated to the French Channel coast with orders to secure the area around Le Havre–Bayeux and to prepare the invasion of Great Britain (Operation Sealion).

(1) Diary, [French Channel coast] 21 September 1940 (BA-MA, N 265/9)

Lieutenant-General Hollidt,[1] our superior, does not believe that there will be an end of the war any time soon. He also does not think that the planned deployments such as the relocation of Army Group B and two Army High Commands [AOKs] to the east[2] will bring peace. I think it is nothing else than leverage towards an ally who has already done things we did not like (Romania).[3] I would not rule out the possibility that in future we will fight a war against 'Bolshevism' as an ideology. What is presently postponed due to reasons of necessity does not have to be cancelled. The strong language in 'Mein Kampf' against Russia is probably not just empty words. The Fuehrer hinted at something of the kind last autumn (1939), when he said that under these circumstances – the western allies had declared war on us – he had to form an alliance with the devil.[4] All in all, there is this one development in the offing: the severity of current events has gained its own momentum and is dragging us into more and bigger ventures, even into those we have never intended in the first place. The first victory involves new problems that will consequently become bigger and bigger. The most difficult thing seems to be finding the right time to finish. The present situation bears a lot of similarities to Napoleon. He advanced on Moscow not of his own choice, but because the war against England forced him to do so.

(2) Diary, [French Channel coast] 29 January 1941 (BA-MA, N 265/10, fol. 56)

Most of our men are in the east. Are they deployed against Russia? That is hard to believe. All transports from there would stop for a long time. Many divisions would be tied up there for years. Or is that, after all, necessary to gain a free hand in the Balkans, which Russia denies us?

(3) Diary, [French Channel coast] 25 March 1941
(BA-MA, N 265/10, fos. 66f.)

We pursue two conflicting interests. One is still in the west . . . Everything is heading to the east, and we will soon, too. That is our second priority. New challenges are awaiting us there. Today Major Knüppel[5] is bringing detailed news about our future from Warsaw. I feel a bit uneasy that there will emerge a new enemy. Three-quarters of the world will then be against us. It seems as if the war against England does always entail a campaign against Russia. It was the same for Napoleon. However, there are substantial reasons for a conflict like this at the present time.[6]

* * *

On 18 April 1941 Heinrici arrived in the Polish district town Siedlce between Warsaw and the Bug River where the General Command of the XXXXIII Army Corps took up their field quarters. The rear quarters were in Tomaszów, southeast of Warsaw. During the days immediately before the German attack against the Soviet Union on 22 June 1941, Heinrici took up his command post near the Bug River, east of Łosice.

(4) Letter to his wife, [Siedlce] 22 April 1941
(BA-MA, N 265/155, fol. 9)

It is not very nice here, bad cold weather, spring is not in sight, bugs and lice are everywhere, just as the awful Jews with the Star of David on their sleeves.

(5) Letter to his wife, [Siedlce] 25 April 1941
(BA-MA, N 265/155, fol. 11)

Tonight we will gain a bit more independence by moving into a house which has been done up as an officers' mess for the *Volksdeutsche* [Poles of German ethnicity]. It consists of two buildings, which are extremely ugly from the outside. Poles and Jews are working like slaves to get everything ready in time. They work day and night. Nobody has any compassion for them here, just like it used to be in ancient times, when the Romans had conquered a foreign people.

(6) Letter to his family, [Siedlce] 30 April 1941 (BA-MA, N 265/155, fos. 13f.)

For almost two weeks we have been in our new area and I have to keep saying: it is such an awful country. It has been raining incessantly for two weeks, and when it does stop once in a while, it is foggy with a slight drizzle coming down in fine raindrops. There is nothing green around here. The trees are still bare, some willows are beginning to green and today I saw some anemones. It is not surprising that the country is not making any progress and that spring will not come, given the constant lack of sunshine. The panjes [small farmers of eastern European countries; transl. note] are still wearing their sheepskins, and right they are. The women have bare legs, with no shoes and stockings, the men wear high bootlegs. The dirt is beyond words. One cannot step out of the house without boots. The so-called causeways have a muddy surface on which the cars slip and slide like on soap. It is extremely dangerous to overtake another vehicle. One could get rather low-spirited in view of this weather and these circumstances, if there was not so much work to do which keeps me distracted. On top of that, there are all these destroyed cities that no one cares to rebuild again, half burnt and overcrowded with people, many more people than during peacetime. Eight, sometimes even eighteen, people are said to share one room. This General Government really is the scrapheap of Europe. And what the houses look like! Half ruined, rotten, dirty, with shreds of curtains at the windows, filthy. When looking into one of these rooms, one can see a complete mess of dead wood furniture. It feels as if we attract lice and fleas merely by walking through the streets. In the Jewish quarters it stinks so much that we have to blow our noses and spit out in order to get rid of the inhaled dirt.

Six days ago we were accommodated in the so-called German House (*deutsches Heim*). That is a kind of hotel, which has been set up by the District Captain for the Germans who work here. The interior of two *Judenhäuser* [Nazi term for houses in which Jews were forced to live] which were still under construction – they are not even plastered from the outside – have been rebuilt by an SS architect and furnished with self-designed high-quality furniture made in Warsaw. The barrooms are something in between a farmhouse and a plain hotel, bedrooms are similarly furnished, but with new and clean stuff. For me the architect has designed a little apartment with a living room in light-coloured pine, bedroom, bathroom and a room for my orderly.

The whole thing is not large but quite comfortable, some kind of a nice lieutenant's flat in which I feel very cosy.

(7) Letter to his family, [Tomaszow] 9 May 1941 (BA-MA, N 265/155, fol. 15)

Last night General von Gienanth[7] invited me to Spala, the former hunting lodge of the Tsar. What I learned about the situation in Poland did not sound very promising. But tomorrow the Governor General[8] will visit. The Jews have to erect flagpoles everywhere to welcome him and build green walls out of fir sprigs to cover up ugly spots. Poles are entitled to 100 grams of meat a week, Jews to nothing. No one really knows what these people live on. It is equally uncertain what will become of this country in future.

(8) Letter to General von Selle, [Tomaszow] 15 May 1941 (BA-MA, N 265/35, fos. 24–6)

After 26 years I revisited Rawa.[9] I came from Tomaszow, i.e. from the south ... This town too has changed a lot over the years. The Poles eradicated all Greek churches to destroy every hint of Russia, root and branch. In Rawa they turned one into a Roman Catholic church. Yet overall, the old Jews' nest [*Judennest*] was still the same, apart from the fact that the Jews, who were so much trouble for our town commander Major Jacobi, are not allowed to run free but are confined in a ghetto.

(9) Letter to his family, [Siedlce] 17 May 1941 (BA-MA, N 265/35, fos. 27–30)

Poverty and misery are indescribable in this country. Cities are worst hit. Half of them were destroyed during the war in 1939. The remaining civilians live in the other half, together with 50 or 60 per cent more people from the province of Poznan, from the Warthegau or from wherever; people are shunted off because they are Jews or other undesirable persons. Eight to twenty people are said to share one room. One can imagine how it must look in there. Houses and flats are still like the war has left them. Windows are covered with wood or cardboard, if they still exist; they have dirty rags for curtains. Shells and bombs have left their marks all over the walls. Jews and children in rags are still searching the ruins for something useful. When it rains, the streets turn into greasy mud immediately. When it is dry, dust fills the air. One cannot help inhaling the dirt with every breath. When walking through the narrow alleys, unimaginable odours of poverty and degeneration mingle with the smell of dirt.

The people here are as miserable as the village is, with clothing shabby and depraved. Probably only very few can afford to buy new clothes. There are some pathetic figures, who literally go about in rags, with trousers and jackets in tatters. Among them there are beggars with missing limbs loitering in the streets and around churches. They are sometimes appalling.

The Jews here are gathered in a ghetto.[10] They wear a white armband with a blue star. In smaller towns the ghettos are not separated from the other parts of the village. Only in Warsaw, a 3m high wall with barbed wire and pieces of broken glass hermetically seals the area of the ghetto. In smaller towns the Jews run free and are used as workers; sometimes they are indispensable as craftsmen. It is typical for this country that when one is in need of something which is not available, one can only get it from a Jew. And he is always and immediately willing to provide it. He does not strain himself with manual work though. He has no holidays. He digs Saturdays and Sundays, but he only works, be it as road or as construction worker, when he is watched. Otherwise he takes a break as I can observe very often from my window.

The population's food supply is about as bad as their clothing. In our town, bread rations for Poles are cut to 75 grams, for Jews to 65 grams. Poles are said to get 100 grams of meat a week, Jews even less. It is all the more surprising that these people are still alive. The Jews are said to have hoarded stocks, which have enabled them to stay afloat until now. However, even these supplies are running lower and lower. It does not bear thinking about what will happen then. Recently I saw a funeral procession. A Jew was borne to his grave. Since the people did not have a coffin, they put the corpse on a tarpaulin fixed on two poles, covered it with a blanket and brought it to the graveyard. ...

Compared to others, farmers are far better off. They are self-sufficient and have no food worries. They live under primitive conditions typical for this country, and their small panje huts fit much better into the landscape than the disgusting and ugly towns with their misguided urban-like buildings. Nowadays farmers get quite a lot of money for the products they have to hand in. They get fertilizer for their fields. Therefore they are more open towards us than the city folk. They greet us saying (with a strange accent): 'Ail Itler.' ... Our soldiers are quite happy with their quarters in the villages. The panjes move into the stables and the soldiers into the houses. The house bug is widespread and dreaded by many. Lice have been seen only sporadically. Thus there are only a few cases of typhus. . . .

By the way, the authorities do not spare the Poles. They made them work from 6am until deep into the night to get the 'German House' ready to move in. The Jews get nothing for their work, they are paid by the Jewish congregation. I do not know if the Poles are being paid. Unsurprisingly, it was all a big mess in the beginning, many things did not work properly and half of them were broken or unusable as soon as they were finished. Yesterday, the District Captain organized a little party in order to check if his guest rooms were fit for purpose. I left at about 11pm. In the hallway I saw four sinister-looking civilians leaning against the wall. When I asked what the Poles were doing here at night – people I do not want to see even in daytime – I was told that they were builders. Apparently, the architect had told them to stay in case something broke. Thus they were standing there waiting. 'It seems as if we do develop into a master race', said one of my companions.

That's what it looks like here. I do not think we have many friends among the Poles. This country, which has been invaded four times within twenty-five years by different armies, seems to be completely destroyed. How things will work out here I have no idea at all at the moment. Without doubt, these are not favourable conditions for the future.

(10) Letter to his wife, [Siedlce] 10 June 1941 (BA-MA, N 265/155, fol. 29)

Kluge[11] visited us for two days, Brauchitsch[12] is coming to Warsaw the day after tomorrow. There is a lot going on.

(11) Letter to his wife, [Siedlce] 13 June 1941 (BA-MA, N 265/155, fol. 30)

Things are rushing. Every day brings us closer to new events, day and night huge convoys roll east, marching columns are 30 to 50km long. The roads are roaring and opaque clouds of dust cover everything.

(12) Letter to his wife, [German–Soviet demarcation line] 17 June 1941 (BA-MA, N 265/155, fos. 33f.)

I have seen our enemies across the river, building and fortifying their positions. They brought material with lorries and panje wagons. . . . It seems as if the Americans are moving steadily towards the war after all. All German consulates in the USA are said to have been closed recently.[13] If they really enter, we have reached World War no. 2. Then we will see how long the whole thing will last. We are probably right at the beginning of great events. Everything is prepared with best efforts.

(13) Letter to his wife, [German-Soviet demarcation line] 21 June 1941 (BA-MA, N 265/155, fol. 36)

When this letter leaves, the new campaign has started. It is meant to eliminate a neighbour who might jeopardize our war against England – be it at the Suez Canal or on the island itself. Besides, it is meant to get us agrarian areas, which can provide us with food supplies sufficient enough to feed the whole of Europe. The latter seems to be the main concern, after America is unofficially at war with us. To some extent, ideological differences also play a role here.

Nobody knows what to expect of the new enemy. During the war against Finland[14] the Russian leadership has proven to be rather poor. The common soldier is probably not a weak opponent as he has shown at the beginning of the Great War. The troops' spirit over there is said to be rather optimistic.

During the last weeks huge numbers of men and materials have been passing by here. The instruments of power on display are enormous. One hopes for a quick decision. It would be most desirable if that happened.

* * *

On 22 June 1941 the XXXXIII Army Corps, including the 131st, 134th and 252nd Infantry Divisions, crossed the River Bug near Mielnik. It formed the southern flank in the battle of Bialystok and advanced further towards the east. In the double battle of Bialystok (until 1 July) and Minsk (until 8 July) the Red Army lost 324,000 men as prisoners, 3,300 tanks and 1,800 artillery pieces. Until 4 July Heinrici's corps was part of the 4th Army (Kluge), then of the 2nd Army (Weichs).

(14) War report to his family, [east of the River Bug] 23 June 1941 (BA-MA, N 265/155, fol. 38)

Yesterday there was a Russian division opposite us, which we took completely by surprise until it was scattered. There are lost soldiers everywhere in the vast forests and at the numerous farms, who often shoot from behind. The Russian is a deceitful soldier in general. Consequently, our men have cleaned up among them on various occasions, without mercy. . . . Everywhere, our men take horses away from the farmers for our carriages, which causes wailing and howling in the villages. That's how the population is 'liberated'. But we need horses and the farmers will probably get some money afterwards.

(15) War report to his family, [east of the River Bug] 24 June 1941 (BA-MA, N 265/155, fol. 39)

Two days ago it started to become boiling hot. The only possible routes of transportation are sandy roads covered in ankle-deep dirt. Every step, every moving vehicle stirs up impenetrable clouds of dust. The marching roads are marked by yellow-brown clouds in the sky. Humans and horses alike suffer extremely under the heat. With every halt, the men fall to the ground like flies and sleep in the small shade of the vehicles, amidst the dust. Their faces are not just dusty but covered in a crust of sand.

At 10.00am I was with the army in Kamieniec. Field Marshal von Kluge gave us marching destinations, which were extremely difficult to achieve due to weather conditions and especially because of insufficient supplies that cannot get over the Bug bridges. Yet with the utmost effort of will we were able to accomplish our objective this evening. We have managed to get from the River Bug near Mielnik to the northeastern edge of the Bialowieza forest within three days. The advanced detachments were even faster. That is a tremendous achievement, although many troops are still waiting for their field kitchen and live on their iron rations. To be sure, the country has to provide a lot. Numerous chickens, pigs and calves have lost their lives. Bread shortage is looming, as supplies cannot get through, because the poor pioneer bridges are still crowded with combat vehicles. The divisions spread over a range of almost 100km in depth. . . .

By and large, the Russian seems to move his forces to the east. If challenged to battle, he is a tough opponent. He is a much better soldier than the Frenchman. Extremely tough, devious and deceitful. Some of our losses are caused by Russians shooting our men from behind. The prisoners we have taken, so far only a few hundred, are from many ethnic origins. Among them, people who look Chinese rather than Russian.

(16) War report to his family, [Lyskow] 4 July 1941 (BA-MA, N 265/155, fol. 40)

The war in Russia is extremely bloody. The enemy has suffered losses previously unknown in this war. The Russian soldiers were told by their superiors that they would all be shot by us. Instead of surrendering, they shoot every German from behind. This provokes countermeasures on our part in return, which are quite severe. This process is escalating with the result that hecatombs of people lose their lives. On top of that the unclear terrain: everywhere forests, swamps, high crops with hidden Russians. In short, it is not exactly pleasant here.

The day before yesterday, after we had cleared the forest and taken 4,000 hidden Russians prisoner, I drove on an embankment in the swamp. On both sides were thick alder bushes. The swamp to the right and to the left was knee-deep. Suddenly a Russian with a rifle in his hand jumped across the road about a hundred steps in front of us. After only a few seconds, seven or eight guys like him followed. No one could tell if there were even more of them. For them it was child's play to shoot us in the car on this road. It was ten of them, three of us. They were hidden in the bushes, we were exposed in the open. For a minute we discussed what to do. The forest was quiet. Just by chance, two of our own vehicles – our reinforcement – drove by. Now we went against the Russians. Yet we could not find them. They were hiding in the impenetrable swamp.

Eight days ago we arrived at our combat position. During the last two days we organized our troops and gave them a rest. Tomorrow we are advancing further to the east, into the Russian heartland. The fight is still not won yet. But the enemy is crumbling.[15] The Russian aeroplanes have not shown up in days. That is a great advantage. …

We still have chickens and eggs and calves. But it will not be long and the country will be sucked dry.

(17) Letter to his wife, [Lyskow] 5 July 1941 (BA-MA, N 265/155, fol. 62)

We took quarters at a chemist's owned by an old Jew. He is happy that he got rid of the Bolsheviks. Apparently, they have treated all people with property really badly. We have seen quite a few big farms and estates. All owners have been eliminated by the Bolsheviks, the farms are neglected, destroyed, abandoned and in a terrible state. They had served as barracks for workers or as hut camps. The Russian soldiers do not seem to be enthusiastic Bolsheviks. The prisoners primarily complain about poor provisions and that their superiors have treated them badly. Apparently there is no real *Volksgemeinschaft* [people's community]. Since the commissars prevented soldiers from defecting and forced them at gunpoint into battle, the soldiers beat the commissars to death in return.

(18) Letter to his wife, [Kozow] 6 July 1941
(BA-MA, N 265/155, fol. 63)

After having finished our battle, we advance to the east in short marches. Because the troops are crowded together, the advance is slower than we would like. The unbelievable state of the roads comes on top of that. Dear Lord, this is a sinister country, north of the Prypiat swamps. It is one huge forest with miles and miles of swamps in between where one sinks knee-deep in mud. It looks much better from above. Yesterday, I flew over my marching columns with the Storch,[16] and everything looked like lovely toys.

The Russian, who was right in front of us, is now destroyed. The whole incident was incredibly bloody. In some cases we gave them no quarter at all. The Russian was like a beast towards our injured soldiers.[17] In return, our men shot and beat to death everything in brown uniforms. The vast forests are still full of scattered soldiers and fugitives, some of them unarmed, some armed, and they are extremely dangerous. Even when we send divisions through these forests, tens of thousands of them manage to avoid capture in this impassable terrain.

Stalin has given orders to the retreating troops to destroy everything we could benefit from.[18] Thus, pillaging and burning as in Napoleonic times, and to some extent as in 1915, is on again. According to my superior Colonel-General von Weichs[19] only two Soviet pomp buildings are left in Minsk, a city with a population of 200,000. Everything else is burnt. In Kozow, where our quarters are, one third of the houses are left. Red commissars have burnt the city centre. The population is probably fed up with this, it is the fourth time for them since 1915!

In the south things are not as good as they are here at the Centre front section. In the Ukraine the Russian retreats orderly and systematically. Thus he is probably able to destroy lots of things. He is too strong to be overrun. His next huge defensive position seems to be at the River Dnieper.

(19) Letter to his wife, [Lyakhovichi] 8 July 1941 (BA-MA, N 265/155, fol. 64)

Leaden sky, 40°C as they say, impenetrable clouds of dust, deep sand, these are the features of the day. Today I drove to the army group next to us and told Field Marshal von Bock[20] about our battles. He said they were among the toughest of this campaign so far, maybe the most difficult ones. Well, I must say I have noticed that. Now we have fallen far behind. We march 30 to 35km [about 20 miles] every day; we can hardly force the horses through the sand, but we need to go further. Since our motorized forces fight 200km in front of us, on their own, they might be able to overpower the Russian without our help. Then we have to walk even further.

This afternoon we had our first bath. It was pure pleasure. The village where our quarters are, Lyakhovichi, is located in one of these typical swamp valleys with a little river. Our soldiers already have a tan and wear only swimming trunks in this heat when they are at rest. Be it in the city centre or elsewhere, there are naked men everywhere. Today we had to execute a Communist woman who had treated injured Russians behind our backs and operated against us with all possible means. That is the war. The day before yesterday, Balzen[21] found the first house bug on my trousers. I live in rooms without any furniture. It is all so shabby and rundown, it is indescribable.

(20) Letter to his wife, [Lyakhovichi] 8 July 1941 (BA-MA, N 265/155, fol. 65)

The roads are littered with the wreckage and debris of destroyed Russian combat vehicles and lorries, cannon, ammunition, decaying horses. The terrain is getting vaster and vaster. Forests and more forests, miles and miles of swamps in between, a few isolated villages. It is always the same, the same image. We still find scattered Russians in the forests. But nobody knows how many are still in there hiding. It is impossible to search these forests and swamps. The scattered Russian soldiers only want to go home as civilians and be farmers again. They do not want to be taken to Germany as prisoners and do not bother about the war.

(21) Letter to his wife, [Kapyl] 11 July 1941 (BA-MA, N 265/155, fol. 66)

Again two marching days. Both boiling hot with indescribable amounts of dust; the troops are utterly exhausted. Yesterday one regiment walked 54km [33.5 miles], another 47km [29 miles]. It is possible to do that once. But if the troops have already done various marches of 30 to 40km before and are expected to do the same afterwards, then these efforts are huge. Besides, no one really sleeps properly during the night. At 2.00 or 3.00am we head off and march until night, sometimes until 10.00pm. Even if there is a rest at midday, we usually have no water and must stay in the blistering sun. Lucky the one who finds a little river. Then everyone tears their clothes off and jumps into the water even if it is dirty. Water is a godsend.

We are now in real Russia. Kapyl is the name of the village today. Everything is completely rotten. We learn to know the blessings of Bolshevik culture. Furniture is very primitive. We usually live in empty rooms. Walls and ceilings are covered with painted Stars of David. Churches serve as halls for political meetings. In every village are big party houses to glorify Stalin and Lenin as favourites of the people, of children, women, workers, soldiers, etc. In the cities there is usually a statue of Stalin built from cement in the market place in the centre, very much like the old Hindenburg. There are no shops. The peasants have to work for the community; they receive one third of the harvest in food and 80 roubles annually. A kilogram of butter costs 36 roubles! As payment for his work every comrade was also entitled to some items such as soap, cigarettes, socks, one suit a year (!), which he could get in state depots in every city. That is the Soviet paradise. No one dares to speak openly. Everyone is afraid to talk. They deported children aged fifteen to the mines at the River Don. These children never heard of their families again and vice versa. Some of them – who are now soldiers – we have taken as prisoners. Now the people here hope to get rid of this pressure. It is a great disadvantage that we cannot communicate with them. This is the reason for many mistakes.[22]

In the meantime the Bolshevik is fighting at the River Dnieper. He has already crossed the river at some places. For us it means running, running, running until our tongues are hanging out. I think they will abandon the infantry after the war. Human power and motor power is too much of a difference.

Hartmut[23] is at the River Dnieper. May God help him.

(22) Letter to his wife, [Slutsk] 13 July 1941
(BA-MA, N 265/155, fol. 67)

The heat and the dust are killing us. It gets hotter and more humid every day. We do not feel like eating, just drinking. We try to march only during the afternoon and at night. It is simply not bearable during the day. Today, the heat is so bad that I can hardly write a letter. The sun is seldom out, but the air is indescribably heavy. One does not feel like doing anything. Yesterday I flew to Minsk. Being up in the air at 600m [2,000ft] altitude was pleasant. The view was terrific, endless forests, rivers meandering like earthworms, marching columns smaller than toys. Minsk, half of it destroyed, only a few multi-storey Soviet palaces left, the *Gauleiter* house, the university building, the House of the Red Army. Flaunty, ugly palaces, all of them filled with pictures glorifying Stalin, Lenin, Kalinin and others. . . .

All churches are destroyed, here in real Russia. The crosses have been removed from the steeples. The Greek Catholic church has been destroyed, here in Slutsk. Using the old bricks of the church a *Gauleiter* house is under construction at the same spot. The Roman Catholic church has been turned into a soda water factory. The Protestant church is merged with another factory. As far as we could see, all churches in the villages are turned into fire engine houses or warehouses. Will the wrath of God descend upon the destroyers? Soon we will be involved in the miserable guerrilla warfare and have to tidy up the forest.[24]

* * *

In mid-July the advance of the XXXXIII Army Corps to the east came to a halt in Bobruysk near the River Berezina. The corps became involved in the prolonged positional and defensive combat against Soviet troops who from then on also took the offensive.

(23) Letter to his wife, [Bobruysk] 20 July 1941
(BA-MA, N 265/155, fol. 68)

The Russian is very strong and fights desperately, urged on by his commissars. Combat in the woodlands is particularly bad. All of a sudden the Russian appears everywhere and fires and attacks columns, individuals and messenger vehicles alike. By any standards, the war is really bad here. On top of that, the incredible transport problems, the vast space, the endless forests, the difficulties in communicating with the people, etc. All previous battles were probably child's play compared to the combat right now. Our losses are substantial,[25] they are huge on the Russians' side. ...

The terrible leaden heat has given way to cooler weather. I am still healthy. I do not get much sleep and I face a tremendous amount of mental stress at some times. I have a bath in the River Berezina every day to relax or I take the Storch and fly over the forest between my two groups. It is 75km [around 46 miles] by car and the road is in bad shape.

(24) Letter to his wife, [Bobruysk] 22 July 2041 (BA-MA, N 265/155, fos. 69f.)

Yesterday we forced the enemy, the Russian LXVI Corps, which was advancing towards Bobruysk, to retreat. Unfortunately they were able to escape from the intended encirclement. We did hit them hard, but again it was not a large-scale victory. The troops have let us down a bit. They got a bit moody due to the fierce and unpleasant battles. Russian guerrilla gangs, who are everywhere in the forests, are characteristic for this war. They attack our soldiers individually, but they do not dare to get near bigger units. Yet they also suffer losses when fighting in the forests. The Russians fight deceitfully and dishonestly in all battles. In the cornfields they throw themselves to the ground, pretend to be dead and shoot our soldiers from behind. In return, our men slaughter the Russians without mercy. There is no campaign like the present one.

Yesterday and the day before it took me hours to drive back home. Many miles through the lonely forest, where there had been fighting the day before. That was not exactly pleasant. Our men are physically exhausted. Yesterday I found some of the carriage drivers sleeping like the dead in front of their horses. Tremendous marches, unbelievable roads. No one in Germany can even start to imagine the state they are in. And huge mental stress due to changing circumstances, and the risk for everyone to be attacked from ambushes: these things are more than distressing and have never been experienced before in any other campaign. And no one knows how long this battle will last. There is no sign of an end at the moment, despite all the victories we have won. Hopefully Russian resistance will break down some day; even for them the situation is far from desirable. Quite the opposite, things are indeed looking bad for them. For the second time they were able to break through at several points. But the cut-off troops fight bitterly and it does not seem as if the Russians' will to resist is already broken or that the people want to get rid of their Bolshevik leaders. Currently there is reason to assume that the war would go on, even if Moscow were captured, from elsewhere in this vast, endless country.

(25) Letter to his wife, [Bobruysk] 26 July 1941 (BA-MA, N 265/155, fol. 73)

I can only say that God saved me. The day before yesterday I witnessed an attack when a Russian 10.5cm grenade hit only 25 steps in front of me and knocked me down. I was half deaf for hours. Then Russian tanks appeared behind the command post. And finally the aeroplane, which was supposed to take me back, exploded and burned two steps away from me. That was enough for one morning.

(26) Diary, [Bobruysk] 30 July 1941 (BA-MA, N 265/11)

The enemy opposite us is a surprisingly active and tough guy. He attacked the 134th Division early in the morning, even though not with full vigour. Seventy-five defectors approached us some hours later. It is almost incomprehensible and always the same: on the whole the Russian fights with fanatical tenacity. As an individual he emphasizes his war weariness, his wish to defect, his hatred against the commissars who force him to fight at gunpoint. These two attitudes are not compatible. If the latter is true, the downfall should be near. ...

My corps has to get out of this messy situation. The endless fights in the forests will be the end of the troops. The Bolshevik warfare of pinpricks gets them down; even the best soldier cannot fend off an attack in the forests and the swamps.

(27) Letter to his wife, [Bobruysk] 1 August 1941 (BA-MA, N 265/155, fos. 76f.)

We are still left with our thankless task that no one is enjoying. The Russian Cavalry Corps behind us has got cold feet, but with all these obstacles – the atrocious forests and swamps, the dreadful state of the roads, the exhaustion of the troops, the enormous distances – so many things are not happening which would be a matter of course under normal circumstances. We have all underestimated the Russian.[26] It was always said that his leaders are pathetic. Well, they have proved their leadership skills with the result that our operations have come to a halt and our men fear their deceitful attacks. Every day about a hundred men defect to us. Maybe the whole business will collapse one day with a big blow over there, when the ordinary soldiers do not want to do it any more. They keep saying that they do not want to fight but that they were forced to do so by the commissars. It is all a bit confusing. A tremendous energy ruthlessly mobilizes all their forces and deploys them without mercy. Thus the Russians were far more successful than any other of our former enemies. Our losses are substantial. The campaign against Russia has caused at least the same amount of losses than all other campaigns together.

It is not yet foreseeable how things will work out here. One senses that the Russian is not willing to give up and surrender as the Frenchman did. It is possible that we will experience a positional war deep in Russia during the winter. The mere thought of it makes everyone look forward to that.

The state of the country here is extremely primitive. Bobruysk, a city of 91,000 – most of them have left – is a dump consisting mainly of wooden houses. The high street reminds me of Königsberg and the *Nasser Garten*.[27] There is no furniture. The people have nothing, as everything has been taken from them over the last twenty years. Our interpreters tell us the people are happy that the Germans are here now. There is no doubt it would be a blessing for the whole world if Bolshevism, its methods and repercussions would vanish from the face of the earth. It is awful. It is a disgusting beast, but it is furiously defending itself.

(28) Letter to his wife, [Bobruysk] 3 August 1941 (BA-MA, N 265/155, fol. 78)

We have done our best to prepare everything despite our limited resources. Again the weather was not to our advantage. It is like a washhouse with scattered showers worsening the state of the already poor roads.

We are amazed about how tough the Russian fights. His units are half destroyed, but he stuffs in new men and they attack again. I have not the slightest idea how the Russians do it. The prisoners insist that it is the pressure of the commissars who shoot everyone who does not comply. But this cannot go on for ever to keep the troops in line. Our swift advance has turned into a slow stumble. It is unforeseeable how far into Russia we get this way, as long as resistance is as fierce as it has been so far. Maybe it will collapse one day. At the moment, however, it is all in limbo. ...

Sometimes we think about the winter and what it will bring about. It is almost certain that we will stay here in Russia. It is pretty unlikely that the Bolsheviks will make peace or get rid of Stalin. Thus we will have to spend the winter here being involved in positional warfare along an enormous front line. Nice prospects.

(29) Letter to his wife, [Bobruysk] 4 August 1941 (BA-MA, N 265/155, fol. 79)

There are new crises and unnerving moments every day; we are fed up with Bobruysk. And life here is quite unhealthy. Too much meat and the lack of many other things, too much smoke, little exercise, the nights, again and again interrupted by various incidents, which makes one feel completely shattered the next morning. I cannot stop thinking about our military problems and do not find a way to unwind. It is not nice here.

* * *

On 5 August 1941 the XXXXIII Army Corps again went on to the offensive. Coming from Bobruysk, it crossed the Berezina and the Dnieper Rivers in a surprise attack and was involved in the encirclement of Gomel (ended on 24 August, 78,000 prisoners of war). The victory of Gomel paved the way for cooperation between Army Groups Centre and South in order to annihilate the Soviet troops in the area of Kiev. As early as 21 August Hitler gave a respective order, which temporarily relocated the main focus of the offensive of the Army Group Centre to the south.

(30) Letter to his wife, 9 August 1941 (BA-MA, N 265/155, fol. 80)

On 5 August we attacked the troops opposite us and forced them 40km back. Initially the enemy withdrew, which made the battle easier than expected. We still lost 400 men. That is enough for a combat like that. In the end, a Russian cavalry division tried to break through, but we were able to fend off their attack and they suffered heavy casualties. Since then, lonely horses are running around everywhere. They are of much use for us, as we lost ninety horses yesterday in an air raid by some of our own bombers, which attacked us by mistake. Unfortunately many men died as well. Very unpleasant is this new habit of the Russians to mine the roads, which has already caused a lot of damage. The enemy opposite us, who kept bothering us, is finally completely destroyed and has little combat power left. We were even lucky enough to capture two commanders' cars of a Russian staff with the division clerk. A typist lady with a blue skirt and white blouse escaped at the last moment. The clerk told us that some days ago their division commander had been dismissed due to poor performance and was then appointed to command one of the regiments of his division. ... Tomorrow we will start new battles. The Russian is hit very hard. It is almost a miracle that he again and again finds the strength for resistance despite casualties and losses. Now it is all about who will persevere the longest. Taking into account the ongoing subversion and disintegration, it makes one think that the whole business over there has to break down one day – even though it will certainly take a while. We have seen entire companies defecting. And the dismissal of senior commanders of all kinds of ranks is not a good sign.

(31) War report to his family, [northwest of Gomel] 18 August 1941 (BA-MA, N 265/155, fos. 82f.)

The Russian defeat at Gomel is a severe blow for our enemy who fights with formations that are merely thrown together, who has hardly any compact divisions left and who was forced to leave a not yet fully assessed but considerably large amount of cannon and vehicles in the forests. In operative terms, it is the end of the southern half of the Russians' centre front sector and will have far-reaching repercussions. Thus we can be satisfied with the last ten or twelve days. I had a hard time. We had to solve very critical situations and at times the stress reached a maximum. It is not exactly enjoyable to travel through the vast country, meagrely accompanied, through miles and miles of forests, subjected to the risk of encountering Russians at any moment. The front lines are extended and porous to such an extent that the area is crowded with friend and foe alike. In a critical situation eight days ago I myself took command of a battalion in a state of complete confusion. Two days ago two Russian heavy batteries attacked us. We were driven out of our command post and it was a miracle that only seven were injured. There was much on offer for every one of us and we can only be grateful that everything went well so far. There were many moments when it might have taken a different turn.

I am writing in a tent pitched up near a half-ruined kolkhoz barn, on the edge of a potato field, which was hit by heavy Russian shells at a distance of 200 steps the day before yesterday. But now the cannon are silent and will never fire again. They are left somewhere in the forest and the artillerists are taken prisoner.

The Russian commanding general of the LXVI Corps, my first counter-duellist, was court-martialled at the beginning of August as an order shows that we captured. Yesterday, the second commanding general of the LXIII Corps and two of his commissars tried to escape. When they did not surrender, our men shot them.

Everything over there is heading towards a crisis. The breakdown is looming.

(32) Letter to his wife, [northwest of Gomel] 19 August 1941 (BA-MA, N 265/155, fol. 84)

The first operation period is over. Two Russian corps with seven divisions are destroyed. We ourselves have taken almost 10,000 prisoners, the whole army around 50,000 altogether. There are huge amounts of war materiel, mostly artillery, vehicles, etc., left in the forests. The Russians have driven it in the swamps so that we cannot use it. After the front lines got mixed up in the wake of the encirclement and the enemy formations broke up, there are lots of single Russians or groups of soldiers in the forests again. Numerous Russians try to hide or to avoid being taken prisoner by using hidden paths.

* * *

After the victorious battle of Gomel the General Command of the XXXXIII Army Corps was temporarily redeployed further east to Starodub before moving south to the area north of Chernigov in late August.

(33) Letter to his wife, [near Starodub] 23 August 1941 (BA-MA, N 265/155, fos. 86–8)

The Russian shows a huge amount of resilience despite all his defeats. Yesterday I read the statement of a Russian army commander-in-chief who claimed that they would keep on fighting even if Moscow fell. I assume he is right. There will only be change when the system in Russia collapses from the inside. I doubt that the preconditions are met yet. It seems as if the dreadful Russian terror system silences every opposition. In the wake of our unexpected attack on Russia, it is plausible that many Russians, even those opposing Stalin, have changed sides and support their leader out of patriotism. . . .

We are now deployed at a different position within our army, with different divisions. We have moved almost 200km deeper into Russia. The cities are all *utterly* burnt. We are camping – one cannot call it 'living' – in the bleakest and most desolate villages. Today I am staying in a classroom, since schools are usually the cleanest buildings. All the houses are really shabby. According to the inhabitants, it is their intention to make everything look ugly and poor so that they are not persecuted for being wealthy. . . .

The war here costs us. Was it really necessary?

* * *

From its new operational area north of Chernigov, the XXXXIII Army Corps slowly fought its way south. It was finally ordered to advance southeast via Kiev, which had been captured on 9 September, in order to keep the envelopment going and to set up the encirclement of Kiev. As early as 17 September – before the end of the operation to encircle Kiev on 25 September (665,000 prisoners, 884 tanks, 3,436 cannon) – the General Command was withdrawn.

(34) Letter to his wife, [north of Chernigov] 1 September 1941 (BA-MA, N 265/155, fol. 89)

Since a couple of days ago we have been in heavy combat again. We have been redeployed south again and are at the northern border to the Ukraine. Our task is difficult, all the more so in light of our limited forces. The Russian fights back with huge resilience and counter-attacks. His artillery is particularly good. I can hear the grenades hitting the ground while I am writing this letter. The day before yesterday the Russian kept us under heavy fire for a quarter of an hour. On top of that, bombers were flying raids on our village and caused several losses, including the commander of the headquarters. It is hard to find time and inner peace to write. The situation is continuously changing and there are always new challenges coming up. This has been going on incessantly for ten weeks. The one I admire the most is the ordinary infantryman who endures everything here, day and night, without having proper quarters. At least the weather is quite pleasant. It has been continuously warm apart from only a few days during the entire summer. . . .

I am convinced that this war will last a long time. There will not be an end of it this year. The Russian hopes for the winter. During this period he will reorganize his damaged army and attack again in spring by command of the English and at his own wish. The English and Americans are happy that the National Socialists and Bolsheviks weaken each other and hope that they will no longer be a threat. Anyway, we have to prepare ourselves for another year of war.

(35) Diary, [Baklanova Morawiecka] 11 September 1941 (BA-MA, N 265/11)

Meeting with the Commander-in-Chief of the 2nd Army, Colonel-General von Weichs. New operation against Kiev. The Army Group [Centre] withdraws the XIII Corps with the best two divisions from the priority flank which forms the northern pincer. The Army Group Centre is not interested in the situation of the Army Group South. Instead it is giving orders to hurry up. Our troops are dead tired, exhausted and weakened. These people over there are short-sighted, they only think of their own operation. This is our perspective. Everyone involved is speechless in view of this decision. And then, the Army High Command [AOK] 2 remains with the Army Group Centre, but relies on the cooperation with Army Group South. One can only shake one's head. I told the senior commanders of the army to give the troops a rest for a couple of days, they would show their gratefulness with a better performance. Everyone who knows the business agrees. Our army tries to do its best in this regard.

(36) War report to his family, [near Chernigov] 12 September 1941 (BA-MA, N 265/155, fos. 92–6)

The state of the Russian troops that we encountered has without doubt worsened lately. In particular the Russian infantry is a wild chaotic bunch of units scratched together, which are thrown into battle as they go along. Regiments filled with hardly trained replacements, divisions consisting of the rest troops of two or three former ones are commonplace. Panzer corps act as infantry without tanks, airborne brigades have nothing to land with. Nevertheless, we still encounter masses of people with our weakened units. Someone once said that if out of a thousand shooting idiots only fifty hit our men, then we will suffer more from these losses than the enemy. Alas, the Russian artillery is very good. They shoot well, have lots of hits and are unfortunately very versatile. The pilots are also dashing and fly in the worst weather conditions. It was not until our fighter aircraft shot down fifteen of them that we had a bit of relief. We Germans particularly dislike the Russian's deceitful way of combat. He is rarely seen in the open country and if so, then only hidden in cornfields. Most of the time he crawls through the forest, through bushes and through the swamps. The Russians attack from ambushes, these people are glued to the unclear terrain like lice and one cannot get rid of them even by combing the area twice. Thus combat here is more than challenging for our troops. One has to raise one's hat to them and their efforts. They have been attacking for eleven weeks, sometimes in the morning, sometimes at midday, and always in front of the enemy, every night outside, not knowing if the brown guys are coming or not, this tension, every day being shot by big, nasty grenades, every night outside in the wet cold, in the meantime walking through knee-deep mud or being completely covered in dust, the effort is utterly great. No one can imagine how much we demand from our soldiers, unless one has experienced it oneself.

The attitude of the Russian military leaders is inexplicable. They do things we cannot comprehend and which seem to be quite unreasonable. For instance, everyone who does not hold his position is going to be shot dead. When we asked the Russian chief of staff [of the LXIII Corps] why he did not withdraw his corps when there was still time, he answered: He had requested it twice of his army commanders. (No one over there is allowed to do anything on their own responsibility; they have to ask their superiors for permission.) His army left his requests unanswered and sent the messenger back. That is how the military leaders avoid responsibility! As a result the Russian LXIII Corps stayed at Gomel and was lost. In a similar manner, some of our own divisions were caught in a completely senseless position. The people over there have the choice of being killed either by a court-martial, by a commissar or by the Germans. The commissars keep telling their troops *every* day for hours that we will definitely not only shoot them, but torture them first. That is why the Russian soldier defends himself so desperately, because he expects to be killed in an even crueller way by us. These primitive people believe everything.

Besides, the prisoners are convinced that Russia will continue this war even if we reach the River Volga. According to them it is a question of life and death for Bolshevism and compromise is not an option. There are enough people. And it is true, we have only seen old men, women and children in the occupied territories. All men are taken and turned into soldiers or factory workers. I am also convinced that the tough willpower of the leaders on the other side will do everything to keep going. They hope, in particular, for the winter, which will hinder us and give the Russians time and opportunity to reorganize. The only logical consequence for us is to hit the Russians hard before the roads become impassable so that their forces are severely damaged and reorganization becomes – at least – a difficult task due to the new losses. I would like to think that is possible. The state of the enemy army and the leaders' often strange fallacies give cause for hope. All the more if we can eliminate the armaments industry on an even larger scale – which is not at all impossible.

For two weeks we have been in the Northern Ukraine, nor far away from Kiev. On the map the country is separated from Belarus by a proper border, the terrain is marked by the destruction of almost all linking roads. There are only a very few major roads, and all by-road bridges are destroyed. The weather is still warm, the roads are finally solid. Instead of being sandy like in Belarus, they are clay here in the Ukraine. The people are better dressed. For weeks we have seen women running around with bare legs, here they wear high boots. The villages are at least 2km in diameter, sometimes even 8 to 10km. They are surrounded by tobacco and sunflower fields (again a popular hiding place for Russian soldiers). Everyone chews sunflower seeds, we too. We have seen large quantities of cattle – as elsewhere, by the way, since we have crossed the German border. Pigs are running freely in the streets and in the houses – often infected with trichinosis. There is no shortage of crops, even though the soil is not cultivated as productively as it could be by our standards.

Thus we hope to get a lot out of the conquered territories during the next season. At the moment we feast on honey, which we have in abundance. Chicken and entire geese flocks populate the vicinity of the villages. In my opinion the kolkhoz system has an advantage: big fields similar to our system of land tenure supersede a system of small fields owned by single peasants. This is a more efficient way of feeding the population. But when we occupy a village, the first thing the village folk ask is: When do we get our land back that has been taken away from us?

Apart from that, everything here is in a terrible and desolate state. Everybody tries to display a poor lifestyle in order not to be persecuted or shot as a property owner. Consequently houses and flats are mostly beyond description. A peasant who has not joined the kolkhoz system but wants to work on his own account (this is possible when farming on a very small scale, i.e. on a property which feeds one cow) does not get any straw for his roof and no timber to mend his house and barn, and has to pay a huge amount of fees of all kinds to force him into the system. This leads to severe poverty. Even worse, however, is the people's fear of the party and its representatives. No one dares to do anything on their own responsibility, but waits for an order so as not to be punished. Thus they started cutting hay only when the order to do so was given – regardless of the weather. One can imagine the damage caused in agriculture by this amount of bureaucracy. There is only one thing of high quality here in Russia: the school buildings. They are huge, bright, spacious and clean without exception. Down to every little village, schools are well equipped with teaching material for physics. We take up quarters only in school buildings because it is the best accommodation possible.

Recently we have been in a village called Szjednjew at the River Snow, where once a Cossack prince ... owned a huge estate of around 240,000 *morgen* [150,000 acres]. Now the palace is completely empty, ruined and run-down. A lecturer from Königsberg named Beutelsbacher,[28] born in the Ukraine and now working as a lieutenant in our intelligence section, had visited the estate with his parents when he was a child and told us about the wealth of the palace, the wonderful park (now a jungle), the library with valuable manuscripts and the lavish lifestyle. None of it was left. Only an age-old lime tree was still there, 400 years old, knobby and gnarly, and next to it the bust of the Ukrainian national poet who used to live with the prince's family 250 years ago. *Our* soldiers beheaded the statue because they thought it was Stalin!

(37) Diary, [near Chernigov] 13 September 1941 (BA-MA, N 265/11)

We came through Chernigov yesterday, arguably the city that has been hit the hardest by the destructive forces of the war. Literally everything is in ruins. Only some churches are left, but their interiors are completely destroyed. Such a destruction of the cities as in this eastern war is probably comparable only with the Thirty Years War.

Colonel-General von Schobert hit a mine and was killed.[29] Manstein is his successor.[30] Schobert was not a bright man, but very ambitious and vain, yet also very brave.

(38) Letter to his wife, [Hotinivka] 15 September 1941 (BA-MA, N 265/16, fos. 70f.)

The war has severe battles in store for us in autumn and the decisive battle has not been fought yet. Certainly the Russian is weak. But the last hit, which will hopefully substantially decimate him, is still to come. Yet I do not believe that Russia will surrender before this winter, even if we win this decisive battle. The country is so huge, there are so many people. For the time being the Russians pin their hopes on

America's and England's help. Both will do their utmost to support this ally, who is a crucial pillar in their fight. The Russian has tied up the entire German Wehrmacht and has caused it considerable casualties – among them the best. You should see how tired and exhausted our troops are. Three months of terrible fighting and marching have left their marks on them. We cannot hope for an end to this campaign and there is no way that we will get leave in the autumn. You have to bear that in mind. The fighting in Russia will go on until the weather puts an end to it.

(39) War report to his family, [Hotinivka] 15 September 1941 (BA-MA, N 265/16, fos. 72–4)

We are just about to encircle the Russian. All troops west of Kiev will bite the dust. For some reason I cannot comprehend, the Russian has assigned his troops in the Ukraine in a way that invites us to take them all prisoners. The encirclement is getting tighter. In a week there will probably be a special announcement declaring another substantial victory. Apart from its military impact it is also very important in economic terms, since new vast areas of the Ukraine – the most valuable part of Russia – will fall into our hands. Our interpreter insists the Ukraine could feed the whole of Europe. Russia would starve without the Ukraine. I am fine with that. Overall these victories are a result of our battles since 4 August, when my corps started attacking in the area south of Bobruysk. These were the first steps and now we will finalize it. We are already positioned deep in the back of Russia's most southern army group. We already fight for the roads that will be essential for the enemy's retreats. While I am writing this I can hear artillery fire rolling continuously. The enemy puts up tough resistance. Yet slowly but steadily he is driven back, leaving one position after another, until he is finished after all.

We will not stay here for the final battle. After having initiated the encirclement and half achieved it, we will be pulled out and redeployed elsewhere. We are not pleased about that. Like everyone else we would rather have completed what we have been preparing for for months. The encirclement of Kiev would have been the capstone of these efforts. Apart from that we would rather stay here in the south instead of moving to colder parts of the country. . . . And we fear that it will be much more inhospitable there than it is here, since for mid-September the weather is reasonably good. The nights are getting cooler, but the daytime can be really hot. The whole country is much cleaner, friendlier and better equipped than forbidding Belarus. . . . The churches in the Ukraine still have crosses; in some remote areas even the interior furnishing has survived. It seems, overall, as if the Bolshevization of the country has not been as intensive and far reaching as in the rest of Russia. A small remnant of independent life has remained.

* * *

On 17 September Heinrici's General Command was pulled out of the encirclement battle of Kiev. He was allowed some days of rest in Chernigov before being redeployed on 23 September to the region northwest of Bryansk in order to take part in the offensive against Moscow.

(40) Letter to his wife, 17 September 1941
(BA-MA, N 265/15, fos. 75f.)

You have caused me great inconvenience. Balzen came back yesterday. He was supposed to bring my old uniform fur coat from Münster. But you have taken the coat to Freiburg and now I am without a fur coat. And today is the first day with cool, autumn-like temperatures making us shiver. I did not expect that in this area, so close to Kiev. But it is true. Now I have not the slightest idea how to get hold of my fur coat. And we are about to move 350km north where it will be even more inhospitable.

(41) War report to his family, [Chernigov] 19 September 1941
(BA-MA, N 265/16, fos. 78–82)

We are in Chernigov, in Russian barracks. At night the bugs dive-bomb us from the ceiling. After having been under continuous stress since 22 June, this seems like a holiday even under these circumstances.

Chernigov used to be a city worth seeing, with formerly 150,000 inhabitants. Now it is literally a heap of rubble. The scale of destruction in the Russian cities goes beyond everything previously experienced and witnessed. In Chernigov only a few single buildings, which have been randomly spared, and some poor huts at the very outskirts of the city are left. Apart from that the city is a smoking heap of ruins. Church steeples, hundreds of years old, tower over the ruins. Their 2m-thick walls defied even modern grenades. Yet they are completely burned. Even if that is not the case, they are in such a horrendous state of dilapidation, depredation and dirt caused by Bolshevism that one

otthard Heinrici (1886–1971). *(Taylor Library)*

Günther von Kluge, commander-in-chief of the 4th Army, from 19 December 1941 of Army Group Centre. *(Taylor Library)*

Iaximilian Freiherr von Weichs, commander-ı-chief of the 2nd Army. *(Taylor Libary)*

Heinz Guderian, commander-in-chief of the 2nd Panzer Army. *(Taylor Libary)*

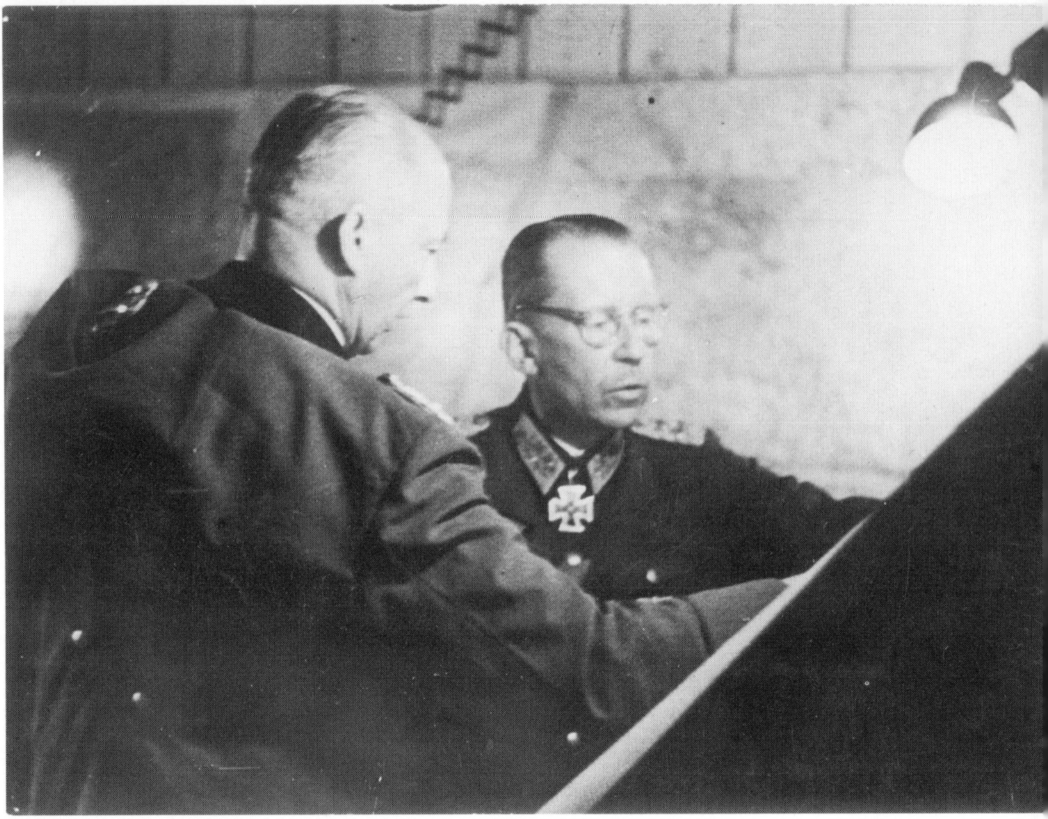

Günther von Kluge (left) with Gotthard Heinrici at a planning meeting. (*Bundesarchiv Bild 146-1977-120-09*

German detachment under lateral fire. 'All of a sudden, the Russian appears everywhere and fires' (20 July 1941). (*Institut für Zeitgeschichte, Munich*)

oviet prisoners, 1941. 'Maybe the whole business will collapse one day with a big blow over there, vhen the ordinary soldiers do not want to do it any more' (1 August 1941). *(Taylor Libary)*

Jative women and German soldiers. 'It is true, we have only seen old men, women and children in ie occupied territories' (12 September 1941). *(Institut für Zeitgeschichte, Munich)*

A city in ruins in the Soviet Union. 'Such a destruction of the cities as in this eastern war is probabl comparable only with the Thirty Years War' (13 September 1941). (*Institut für Zeitgeschichte, Munich*)

erman soldiers resting. 'You should see how tired and exhausted our troops are' 5 September 1941). *(Institut für Zeitgeschichte, Munich)*

oviet soldiers taken prisoner. 'Sometimes he fought bravely as usual, sometimes he scattered into e forest and let himself be taken prisoner' (23 October 1941). *(Institut für Zeitgeschichte, Munich)*

Muddy period in autumn, 1941. 'All our supplies are stuck in the mud and the deep roads' (27 October 1941). *(Institut für Zeitgeschichte, Munich)*

Peasant and German soldiers. 'We can only get these partisans with the help of the Russian people living here' (19 November 1941). *(Institut für Zeitgeschichte, Munich)*

burning village on the Eastern Front. 'It is like the Thirty Years War, the same habits and customs' 9 November 1941). *(Taylor Libary)*

viet soldiers in Moscow. 'Equipped with phenomenal winter gear, he penetrated the wide gaps in ır front' (22 December 1941). *(Taylor Library)*

Winter on the Eastern Front. 'In early February we had blizzards for three days' (6 February 1942).
(Institut für Zeitgeschichte, Munich)

Thaw in spring. 'Now it has been thawing for a couple of days' (20 April 1942).
(Institut für Zeitgeschichte, Munich)

has to look away in disgust. And it seems as if these churches used to be extremely beautiful once. There are a few that would be objects of interest even in Germany due to their wild baroque features, their size and their strange beauty. Chernigov used to be a pilgrimage city with a particularly miraculous picture of the Virgin Mary. From the cellar of an otherwise completely burned museum I have rescued twenty-five paintings. . . .

The scale of destruction in the cities of this country due to Bolshevism and in addition due to the war goes far beyond the Thirty Years War. In the countryside, on the other hand, the impact of the war is hardly noticeable after only a couple of days. It does not matter how hard the villages have been hit, how many of the poor panje huts are destroyed and how many calves, chickens and piglets with trichinosis have been eaten, the countryside does not change that much overall. Only by considering the details and individual cases can one conceive the destructive power of the war. Probably there will be books written about that matter in the years to come. The cities are almost completely deserted. In the villages only women, children and old people are left. Everyone else wanders around in the vast country of Russia, detached from their homes. According to our prisoners, huddles of people crowd the railway stations and beg pieces of bread from soldiers. The casualties caused by the war among these uprooted people due to sickness and exhaustion are, in my opinion, as high as the bloody losses. Maybe this situation, together with the military defeat, will cause an opposition against the ruling system in Russia one day. However, as I mentioned before, there is no sign of it so far. The Soviets are greatly feared everywhere, their terror is without mercy, so that no one dares to protest. Besides, large parts of the youth are committed Communists who think that these measures are necessary to rule a primitive people like the Russians. Thus we will have to impose on them long-lasting and sustainable pressure until the domestic situation in Russia is so unbearable that it will paralyse their resistance. The loss of the Ukraine, the jeopardized industrial areas around Kharkov, the elimination of Petersburg are steps to this end. . . .

Now that the summer is over and there is no more swimming and bathing, we suffer from a plague of lice, which was dreaded already in the Great War. And again, it is the infantry who are completely lice-ridden, although the men strained the most, have a heavy workload and cannot do much against the lice. We use the current time of rest to deal with that problem as effectively as possible. Our railroad, which surprisingly – without timetables, block system and sometimes with a change of trains – reaches as far as where we are, gives us some delousing days until the troops are transported elsewhere.

At present we dismiss all Russian prisoners from the conquered western territories so that they can return to their hometowns.[31] They are urgently needed there, because there is a lack of agricultural workers. I assume that it is also a preparation for the establishment of new satellite states. The English once presumed we would create an independent Ukrainian state as well as an independent Belarus and Baltic states. Now we are in a position to initiate this.

(42) Letter to his wife, [Chernigov] 20 September 1941 (BA-MA, N 265/16, fos. 82f.)

The day before yesterday the Fuehrer decorated me with the Knight's Cross.[32] The Commander-in-Chief of the Army [Weichs], who was deployed with us in Chernigov for one day, invited me and Schulz[33] unexpectedly for dinner and presented me with the decoration. I was completely taken by surprise. I had not expected anything like it. Well, we must have achieved something useful and important. But I had never thought of anything like that. I am especially happy for Hartmut who will be very pleased. However, I would have preferred not to have been singled out like that in the speech that explained the reasons for the decision.

(43) Letter to his wife, [Chernigov] 22 September 1941 (BA-MA, N 265/16, fos. 83f.)

Yesterday the *Wehrmachtbericht* [armed forces report] listed the numbers of prisoners taken by Reichenau's[34] Army. Our army was not mentioned, even though *we* got him out of a jam in which he had been stuck for six weeks without the chance to move. Only the efforts of *our* army and the tanks have created the preconditions for the encirclement of Kiev. As soon as the encirclement was closed, we were pulled out. Now others show off with the prey we have provided. That spoils the mood, especially for the troops. It is said that we were not mentioned due to reasons of secrecy. I am sorry for our Army Commander Colonel-General von Weichs, who is a quiet and particularly decent man.

(44) Diary, [near Krychaw] 24 September 1941 (BA-MA, N 265/11)

The decisive battle has not been fought yet. Those at the top have been greatly mistaken about Russia. We can only hope that the forthcoming events will push things forward so that we can consider Russia as effectively eliminated. Yet even in this case there is no reason to get our hopes up for a change in the domestic situation in Russia and therefore for its dropping out of the war. England has certainly recovered during this summer. America is impatient to enter the war. The final decision of the war is yet to come. That means it will take a long time.

(45) Letter to his wife, [near Krychaw] 24 September 1941 (BA-MA, N 265/16, fos. 84–6)

We have moved 250km north but have still not arrived in our new section. There are no more sunflower and tobacco fields, only potatoes. The region we are approaching is said to have been the best for wolves throughout the entire European part of Russia. That means it will be again a terrain with forests and swamps involving all consequential difficulties and nasty problems! ...

Since large parts of the Russian Army Group South have been annihilated – thanks not to Reichenau's, but to our own army and fortunately in particular to my corps – the forthcoming events will be essential for the overall development in the east. The more successful the better, since in that case the Russian will not be able to recover until next spring. No one who got to know Russia wants to fight next year as we did this year. Every German who encountered Bolshevism here is sick of it.

The war is still pending. If America enters – which has basically already happened – a new enemy will emerge who can support England at least with its air force and navy.

(46) Diary, [near Krychaw] 25 September 1941 (BA-MA, N 265/11)

Flew to the army at Klintsy with the Storch, 50 minutes' flight, over an armoured train, which has been completely destroyed by our Luftwaffe. Klintsy is a completely preserved city of 40,000, the first undestroyed one we have seen since the German border. How amazing is that. Old wooden churches with artistic icons and a market with stalls in front of it. The city-folk are happy and grateful that they can use their church again. Unfortunately we do not know how to use this advantage by assisting them in repairing the churches.

(47) Diary, [southeast of Roslavl] 27 September 1941 (BA-MA, N 265/11)

Anyhow, our concentration of troops was not disguised at all, not even slightly. Intercepted radio messages from the Russians asking for reinforcement in light of an imminent German attack give a broad hint that they are not blind. But because we are pressed for time we do not bother about that. Our divisions arrive at the last moment, so to speak with their tongues hanging out, from the southwest. The operation should and indeed must start as early as possible, because winter is just around the corner. Still, it would have been possible to disguise the advance by little detours. Because it is not my division I have no say in that.

There is speculation as to whether the Russian Army Group Timoshenko[35] will answer or evade the attack. The overall situation would require that of them. Since we have torn a big hole in their lines at Kiev, Timoshenko cannot stay without jeopardizing their left wing. On the other hand, evading would mean abandoning the area around Moscow and the war industry located there. Now, this as well as Kharkov and the Donetsk Basin are at risk.

(48) War report to his family, [southeast of Roslavl] 29 September 1941 (BA-MA, N 265/16, fos. 86–8)

In the meanwhile it has started to freeze every night. Even during the daytime we have rarely more than about 4 to 5° C. A permanently grey sky lies over the country and a cold wind blows across the fields. People with a good knowledge of the weather insist it will stay like that until late October, then it will rain until mid-November, then the rivers will freeze and thaw at the end of April. Nice prospects!

You at home cannot possibly imagine what it means to live outside day and night, as the infantry have to do. And yet they all wear summer instead of winter clothes. The panjes already wear their sheepskins. They are of a very strange cut: a tight-fitting waistline with a bell-shaped, pleated lower part made out of sheepskin which is worn inside out. The women cover their heads with thick shawls. They all look as if they have toothache. They wear flannel or felt wrapped around their calves and bast shoes. To be honest, they look a bit like Eskimos!

All of this is called Great Russia. That is where we are. There are vast forests in front of us. Wolves are said to be living in there. Rumour has it that a man has already been bitten by a rabid wolf bitch. All that is possible here, not just lice and bugs. We no longer even mention them.

We have not witnessed any poorer villages than these ones. Low and narrow, they are nestled in hollows. They are built out of beams, even on the inside. One feels like a trapper in the Wild West. Oven and hob is the same thing with a big firehole in the middle where the burning logs of wood are. There is no coal. People use wood as fuel. The oven is so big that it extends far into the room. Because it is located at the longitudinal wall, it divides the room into two smaller chambers. There are wooden pallets as beds. A second sleeping place is on top of the oven, which is about 1.5m high. This seems to be the place of honour. I guess we will also sit there if the temperature falls below minus 30°C.

(49) Letter to his wife, [southeast of Roslavl] 29 September 1941 (BA-MA, N 265/155, fol. 112)

We are on the brink of the decisive battle in Russia. We can be optimistic that it will be again a great success. It is not yet certain that it will reach the same proportion as the battle of Kiev. However, the further development of the overall situation in the east relies on our imminent achievements. The situation in Kiev is said to be quite unpleasant, because the Russians have hidden a great amount of mines and incendiary devices which cause lots of detonations.[36] The kind of warfare we witness here has nothing to do with a decent battle.

(50) Diary, [southeast of Roslavl] 1 October 1941 (BA-MA, N 265/11)

In an excellent decree[37] the Fuehrer points out the weight of this decisive battle. Whether our approach meets these expectations in general remains to be seen. We think that it is too shallow and will therefore not result in the desired encirclement of the majority of the enemy. Yet it would be really bad if the Russian were able to get away in large numbers. Then he would still have enough resources to rebuild his army during the winter.

* * *

The attack of the Army Group Centre on 2 October 1941 was supposed to force the breakthrough towards Moscow. Operation Typhoon (Unternehmen Taifun) initially led to German victories in the battle of Vyazma and Bryansk. In the course of this operation the XXXXIII Army Corps crossed the River Desna at Shukowka (northwest of Bryansk) with the 52nd and the 131st Infantry Divisions, advanced on Shisdra and formed the north flank of the encirclement of Bryansk.

(51) Letter to his family, [Bytosh] 8 October 1941 (BA-MA, N 265/155, fos. 155f.)

Back in school again, sitting at a school desk, writing. Outside we have the first snow. The cold autumn wind tears the leaves from the trees around the destroyed church on the opposite side. It is surrounded by the ruins of the smashed tomb of a family who used to be the benefactors of the village. It was probably destroyed twenty-three years ago during the revolution. Nobody cared to remove them. The villa owned by this rich manufacturer family was turned into a party house. Today only the chimneys are left. On the opposite side the ruins of the factory that was burnt down by partisans before the Germans approached are still smoking. A shed filled with firewood also contains the debris of a chopped-up iconostasis, which used to embellish the church. It includes the remains of magnificent ecclesia books and Bibles bound in leather and velvet. Anything beautiful in this country has been completely destroyed by Bolshevism. The few remaining things will finally be destroyed by this war.

On 2 October we have again taken the enemy by surprise with our attack. We would never have thought that this could happen given our openly conducted preparations. The Russian knew neither the time nor the direction of the attack. As a result entire corps were able to march by without getting into contact with the enemy on the first and second day after the breakthrough through the enemy positions – including my own left wing division. Nevertheless, the battle is still going on. We have to expect that the surrounded enemy will try to break out of the encirclement with desperate courage. We have already experienced twice what that means. Yet by and large it must be said that the opponent is already beaten and that he will now lose the remaining core of his army, which is supposed to defend Moscow. At the end of the month he will have neither his capital city nor the famous industrial area of the Donets Basin, and will be left with an extremely weakened army. It will not be easy for the Russian to make good these losses. Yet we cannot assume that the war with him is over. So far every prisoner said: And even if you throw us back to the Ural Mountains, there will be no peace between you and us. The Bolshevik cannot make peace with the National Socialist. An agreement between them is impossible. It is true we are battered, but not beaten yet. We rely on the greatness of our country and on our huge human resources. And on the assistance of England and America.

Therefore we do not know how far we have to fight our way through this forbidding country. Again there are forests, swamps and bad roads everywhere. So far the weather has been favourable during the first days of the offensive. But if it turns wet, we will face great difficulties.

(52) Diary, 10 October 1941
(BA-MA, N 265/11)

Clear skies in the evening, around minus 5°C. Have again applied for light winter clothing. Our men are still wearing their summer uniforms. But the army group has 'categorically' decided that ammunition and food supply are more important than clothing. In my view 'categorical' decisions are mostly wrong. It is always possible to send a few train carriages, which would help a lot. In the current situation no inferior would dare to violate a 'categorical' decision. Even the field post can no longer be delivered, even though there have been *empty* carriages on some trains.

* * *

Even before the end of the encirclement of Vyazma and Bryansk (18 and 20 October, in total 663,000 prisoners), Heinrici's corps advanced northeast to the River Oka, passing Sukhinichi and Kozelsk, and occupied the river valley between Kaluga, Likhvin and Belyov until the end of October. The season of mud starting on 16 October hampered this advance and finally stopped it. From 19 October the XXXXIII Army Corps was assigned to the 2nd Panzer Army (Guderian).

(53) Letter to his wife, [Sukhinichi] 16 October 1941
(BA-MA, N 265/155, fos. 117f.)

Today is our 21st anniversary. And I am here in Sukhinichi, a miserable Russian village southwest of Kaluga. All day long it was snowing, which turned all roads into a black, bottomless swamp. I took the road to Kosiolsk today and could see a long line of sunken, gridlocked and broken lorries, hopelessly stuck. Almost as many dead horses lay in the mud next to the vehicles. We got also stuck today due to the bad roads.

We – that is my corps – have started a new encirclement. For the fourth time in the course of this campaign we have caught up with the withdrawing Russian and cut off his retreat. The enemy army at Bryansk tried to break through where we engaged them. In four days of arduous battles involving heavy losses we have driven them back section after section until we could encircle them completely. Five thousand prisoners and 102 guns were the corps' prey in these early days. We left it to a different corps to finish off the encirclement completely, which did not pose a challenge, and marched northwest. The Russian army is crumbling. Now and then there are clear signs of disintegration. Today I read that London fears a separate peace between Russia and us. I cannot imagine that Hitler will agree to make peace with the Bolsheviks, only with a system friendly to National Socialism. – Just now I hear the message that Odessa has fallen.[38] Our front-line division is only 73km from Moscow! I think there is not anybody among us who does not wish for an end of our war and our stay in Russia. But no one really believes that that will be the case. Everyone would leave this country with the greatest pleasure since it means only hardships, ugliness and painstaking efforts. No one can really imagine what every single man here has to endure in this weather, this terrain, the state of the country and the challenges the war forces on him. Only someone who has experienced this himself can understand what it means to be on watch all night long without warm clothes (for instance without gloves), with wet feet, in the forest without shelter, freezing, without a hot drink, possibly with a hungry stomach. …

Goodbye for today. I hope we can celebrate our next anniversary at home and in peace.

(54) Diary, [Kozelsk] 18 October 1941 (BA-MA, N 265/11)

A particular difficulty for us is not having any decent maps. The so-called old Russian ones are so outdated that hardly anything is right. Where it says forest are in fact fields, the roads are always wrong and half of the villages are missing. Sometimes we can capture maps and these ones are much, much better than our German 1:100,000 scale maps, clear and precise and updated. But at the moment we have not got those, therefore we are half blind.

The landscape has changed a lot. After the lowlands it has become hilly and very lively. It is even more difficult to get up and down on this slippery, muddy surface.

(55) Diary, [Kozelsk] 19 October 1941
(BA-MA, N 265/11)

It has been raining for the whole day. Supplies cannot get through because every vehicle gets stuck. Even at the General Command bread rations are cut. We have found flour in the city and started to bake bread in the kolkhoz bakery.

From now on we are assigned to the Panzer Group Guderian.[39] It is located in Orel. We are not exactly happy about the separation from the 2nd Army, since with the Panzers we are only a fifth wheel. Under the current circumstances and due to the given distances we cannot even reach them. The 2nd Army also regrets us leaving. When I gave notice of our departure over the phone, the Colonel-General [von Weichs] cordially thanked us and mentioned the 'great victories' the corps has achieved. We are also reluctant to separate from the 2nd Army because they have always supported us in the best possible way.

(56) War report to his family, [Kozelsk] 23 October 1941
(BA-MA, N 265/155, fos. 120–3)

I am writing in the barracks of Kozelsk. I may as well tell you that much because it will be weeks given the current field post deliveries until the letter will reach you. Since the resistance of the Red Army west and south of Moscow collapsed, mother nature has taken over to defend Russia. The temperatures of minus 3° to minus 8°C and the light snowfall, which started at the end of September, turned into rain a few days ago. Thus our potential movements are highly restricted, as an example may show: a lorry took thirty-six hours for a distance of 35km. Everyone was thrilled that it arrived at all. Most of the convoys are stuck in deep mud, in the swamp, in deeply rutted roads with potholes half a metre deep, flooded with water. The lorries, which are already in quite a state, are now completely broken (spare parts are impossible to get). Petrol, bread, oats, nothing gets through. The horse carriages are stuck, guns are not getting through, all men, be it infantry or something else, are more pushing than fighting. The roads are covered with dead horses and broken lorries. Again and again the lamentation: it cannot go on any longer! And yet, it has to be done, we have to move on, even though slowly. Panje carriages, the rescuers of the Great War, are again the vehicles the entire transport relies on. But it is nearly impossible to travel distances of 100 or 120km to the supply base and back again with panje carriages, which means that we are facing almost insoluble problems. Thus we are quite happy that it has become a bit colder and windier since yesterday. We hope that at least the roads will dry off. It is thanks to Churchill that we have been delayed for four weeks by getting involved in the Serbian campaign during the spring.[40] We would already be in Moscow, if it had not been for this episode.

In contrast to the landscape we have seen so far, the region around Kaluga, where we have just arrived, is extremely hilly with differences in altitude of up to 60m. Streams and rivers are still and deeply cut into the ground and are the reason for the steep slope of the roads. The heavy clay soil, partly black, turns into soap when it rains. The inhabitants of the country look like Eskimos. They wear bast shoes, patches of felt wrapped around the legs or felt boots; they cover their bodies with an old-fashioned thick brown sheepskin (which protects against bomb splinters), they have thick shawls wrapped around their heads showing only eyes and nose. They share the living rooms of their pitiful sheds with pigs and chickens. They sleep on the oven. Bugs and lice populate the living rooms. 'What a bleak geography,' this is what my captain from Wurttemberg said and I can only agree with him! These people cannot be judged by our standards. I believe it would be better and more appropriate to approach this country not gradually by foot as we do but by ship leaving the home shores, breaking away from everything we are familiar with and discovering it like a foreign, unknown continent. Time and again I ask our new interpreter [Beutelsbacher], a manufacturer's son from Odessa currently working as a lecturer in Königsberg, if and why no one in this country has tried to work against the sloppiness and inefficiency, this indifference. I always get the same answer: The Russian is completely passive, he does whatever he is told to do and is, under guidance, an eager and excellent worker. But he does not undertake anything of his own accord, has resigned himself to the most miserable circumstances and has no aspirations whatsoever to improve them. Rather than taking up his own enterprise and risking hard work and worries, he suffers and starves himself to death. He is content with one pair of shoes for the whole family – which go from foot to foot – if he can avoid work. In winter he only leaves his place on the oven to shovel a footpath from the house to the well through the 1.5m deep snow. After that his zest for action is exhausted. And yet endless resources could be got out of this country. The amount of land which remains fallow. How sparsely populated these endless areas are. The state of the forests, which are neglected not efficiently cultivated. There is no afforestation at all. Trees are cut down as required, as for the rest, it is left to nature if they grow back again. If one asks again: What is to become of this country in future, given the character of the Russian? Do you think that the Russians will abolish the current political system due to the defeats? One gets the answer: They are incapable of doing that of their own accord. There is nobody who would care to do so. There is nothing else for us to do but to set up a government in the occupied territories. They do not love Bolshevism per se. Too many have lost close relatives due to the system. Everyone lives under the constant pressure of fear of being spied on. Peasants want their land back. Old people are longing for their churches (in Chernigov I witnessed an old woman who kneeled in front of us and thanked us because she could attend mass again). All the others think that their economic situation is too bad. Bolshevism has no friends here. But Russia cannot destroy it of its own accord. – And even if we set up a government in the occupied territories, what will become of the unoccupied areas? Nobody can answer that. What you get as an answer is just a shrug and the word: Nitschewo [Nikto]. Nobody knows how things will develop. They probably have their own plans in the Fuehrer's headquarters. I myself do not know what to make of it. …

During the battle the Russian displayed a behaviour which proved his unpredictability. Sometimes he fought bravely as usual, sometimes he scattered into the forest and let himself be taken prisoner. I have come across Russian troops of ten to twenty unarmed men who only wanted to know where to go to be taken prisoners and who thanked me cheerfully when I told them what the closest city was – Shistra. Others came out of the forest with their hands up to surrender when they saw a German. Once they even started to shoot their own men with a battery we had conquered and turned around. Hundreds of them drive panje carriages or lorries on behalf of our divisions. Almost every unit has some Russian soldiers who speak a bit of German and who work as interpreters. The other day two cavalry lieutenants came to us with a cavalry platoon in perfect order, with two vehicles and fully armed. They declared that the Russian side was in such a mess, the entire chain of command and all supplies were impaired (they did not have anything to eat for four days), order followed counter-order, so that they did not see the point in going on fighting. Today a captain on horseback came to us and said that the lack of discipline was so bad that he had rather left this forlorn bunch. That means that they are definitively heading towards a crisis, the huge losses of human resources and materiel are starting to be felt and force the Russian to send untrained men to the front with neither soldierly will nor education. Our aeroplanes drop propaganda leaflets with so called 'passes' which are very much sought after by Russian soldiers who search for and keep them.[41] They beat each other to get one of these 'passes', because every one of them hopes they will get to us where they will not be tortured, as their commissars want to persuade them. They wave the leaflets or get them out of their pockets when they are taken prisoners as evidence that they are only forced soldiers and that they do not want to fight against Germany. But let it be understood, it is not like that everywhere. Besides the tens of thousands of bad Red Army soldiers there are thousands of good ones and they offer, even today, tough and fierce resistance and counter-attacks like yesterday's, when we faced unpleasant consequences and heavy losses. It is of utmost importance to destroy, if possible, the rest of their troops who still offer resistance before the beginning of winter in order to prevent a reorganization of the Russian army during the winter months. For the time being this objective is hindered by strong, still unbeaten units in the northern sector of the Russian Front and also by the strong and well-equipped Far East Army at Vladivostok. I do not know to what extent it is and will be occupied by the Japanese. Therefore we are focusing more and more on the near winter months, which we do not look forward to at all. Lucky are those units which might be pulled out and deployed elsewhere. This will certainly not happen to us!

(57) Letter to his wife, [Kozelsk] 24 October 1941 (BA-MA, N 265/155, fol. 124)

Do not worry about the Christmas presents from Moscow. For the time being the Russian grimly defends himself. A lot of blood will be shed before we get there, but we definitely will. We might go into this nest of communists or let them all starve and freeze to death, instead of bothering with exhausting street fights. We'll see about that![42]

(58) Diary, [Kozelsk] 25 October 1941 (BA-MA, N 265/11)

Everything has stopped due to the wet weather and the roads. Just before we have reached our target, Moscow, we are stuck. Finally we have a ratio of four German against one Russian division. And we cannot use it. For days the motorway to Moscow was completely gridlocked: the 9th and 4th Armies rely on it. Now two rear infantry divisions are assigned to regulate the traffic. And yet the Russian only defends the roads. Between them there is not much. But we, too, can only use the roads for advance. The situation is very unsatisfactory. I told Colonel Blumentritt,[43] my superior: We are missing the four weeks of the Serbian campaign. Yes, he said, and on top of that the three weeks from July to the first half of August that we lost while our superiors were arguing whether our next target would be Moscow or the industrial area Donetsk.[44] Back then we missed weeks of the best possible weather because we were ordered an operational rest. It is true, it was during those unpleasant days at Bobruysk, when there was talk that the supreme leadership was indecisive about what to do. The Fuehrer wanted the industry, Brauchitsch Moscow. Then our battle of Gomel has inevitably paved the way towards the south and we could not avoid it. But even then we thought that the supreme leadership was still hesitating and pursued this new direction only half-heartedly and with insufficient means. And we have to suffer the consequences. Since the only focus of Army Group Bock was Moscow, now they have to pay for their mistakes. The weather prevents an easy victory.

(59) Letter to his wife, [Likhvin] 27 October 1941 (BA-MA, N 265/155, fol. 119)

We have to give up all hope. All our supplies are stuck in the mud and the deep roads, the lorries have no petrol, the men no bread, the horses no oats.[45] In many cases the men do not even know where their lorries are stuck. Since better weather is not to be expected, *our* advance will be very slow. Other units enjoy better road conditions and are only 60km away from Moscow; they will soon be in front of its gates. At any rate the weather has unexpectedly put a spoke in our wheel. This might turn out very badly for us. Nobody dares or is able to imagine the road conditions here. There is a thick paste of mud, 30 to 40cm deep, covering the surface of the roads. It looks like a wave of mud in front of the cars and lorries as long as they are moving before they get stuck. Only a fraction of our freight hold is in fact at our disposal. Under the current circumstances even more lorries break down. We had already left our good passenger cars 60km behind when we changed our position yesterday. We always hope for better weather. But usually there are downpours on the third day after two days of light drizzle.

(60) Diary entry, [Likhvin] 29 October 1941 (BA-MA, N 265/11)

Things are not much different at the Panzer Army. They too have huge difficulties of supply. Depending on the width of the road the 'army' fights with a head of six tanks and one company. Everything else stands behind them on the road to Tula, which is partly destroyed and sunk into mud in many places.

Guderian hopes that we will be able to open up Tula for him by turning eastwards. But we can hardly move ourselves. My main request is: Drop petrol. But the Panzer Army is in no position to 'promise' anything; they, too, can only 'hope'. Thus our visit was of limited success.

What are the war prospects regarding Russia? Like me Guderian fears a hibernation often disturbed by Russian troops, and in the next year a war like the one Japan fights against China.[46]

(61) War report to his family, [Likhvin] 30 October 1941 (BA-MA, N 265/155, fos. 125f.)

Our main opponent is the weather. Despite a few pleasant days, the roads are not drying. . . . Because the lorries cannot get through, we have neither fuel, nor oil nor bread nor coffee, etc. and our stock of ammunition is running low. We have enough meat, cabbage, even potatoes (although not too much). We also have corn, while we are running out of oats. By and large, we are stuck with our vehicles, because we cannot use the roads, which is a precondition for our advance. Nature has beaten technology. We were really lucky that this did not already happen in late September, when we were just about to destroy the Russian Centre Army Group. But what an irony that this halt happens to us at the very gates of Moscow. The divisions are just 60km, three little days' march, away from the capital. We have already reached out our hands for the stronghold of communism, so to speak. We are vastly superior! Yet ten days ago the runner who longs for victory got stuck in mud! . . .

To our surprise we have discovered a silver fox farm close to Likhvin. Our soldiers have already shot ten of the precious animals without rhyme or reason, since the fur is useless at the moment. We were told again that the vast forests, which we have been crossing since 2 October, are still inhabited by bear, wolf and elk. We have not seen any of them. In winter wolves and elk are said to leave the forest and come into the Oka valley. By then we will not be here any more but in Moscow.

The other day I talked to a military commander about what is ahead of us. Well, he said, we will probably be hibernating here, many times interrupted by the Russian. And I replied, and next spring we will have a war here like in China. New armies will emerge here and there which we will have to defeat in a special campaign. That's how it will be, he said.

(62) Diary entry, [Likhvin] 1 November 1941 (BA-MA, N 265/11)

For the second time our aeroplanes have dropped bread. How much help is that? It is like a drop in the ocean. What we need is (1) supplies being transported by train via Kosiolsk, (2) catching up with the motorized troops, (3) petrol.

We will not get all of it. We cannot even get a Storch here. We have no connection to the divisions. We are in a fix, helpless. We have never experienced a situation like this. The weather does not change at all. It is warm and wet all the time. We hope for frost, but it is always raining. Then the roads are impassable at once. We've been stuck in this bloody backwater for eight days. Bugs and lice are our roommates. There is no hope for an improvement of supplies. We live from the land. We bake our own bread. What the men miss most is that they no longer have any drink rations like coffee or tea, and they have to survive on soups. Otherwise they are not too bad. They just eat everything they find here. But this, again, is limited. Some items are already running short, for instance oats.

(63) Diary, [Likhvin] 2 November 1941 (BA-MA, N 265/11)

They have cancelled the Storch again. I was supposed to drive to the 31st Division, which is 120km away. I was not feeling very well. Thus someone younger could go this time. I sent Major Knüppel. He took eleven hours. I cannot see why the younger ones always stay at home and send their generals on twelve-hour trips. Instead visited the aid station of the 131st Division in the afternoon, which was a picture of misery. Terrible air, severely wounded soldiers on straw, one man with pneumonia whose leg has to be amputated, many with gas phlegm. Thank God that we have now the serum, which had not been invented in the Great War. Back then they all had to die. I cheered the men up and thanked them. They all look forward to being home again.

Lieutenant Beutelsbacher killed off altogether twelve partisans, some yesterday in Likhvin, some today nearby. You would not think that this small, unremarkable man has this amount of energy. He takes revenge on Communism for his father, his mother, his siblings, who all died or were exiled under this regime. He is a merciless avenger. Nevertheless, two straying Red Army soldiers killed one of our soldiers at Likhvin. There are people like that everywhere in the forest, together with partisans.

* * *

From 3 November the wet weather turned into a cold snap which allowed the conduct of offensive operations again. They became more extensive after mid-November, but newly formed resistance from the Red Army had to be faced. The XXXXIII Army Corps (now with the 31st and the 131st Infantry Divisions) was assigned by the 2nd Panzer Army (Guderian) to support the advance of the Panzer formations (XXIV Panzer Corps) on Tula from the northwest and to move forward from the Oka area near Kaluga and Likhvin towards Aleksin and further in order to meet the tanks north of Tula and to finalize the encirclement of this pivotal area, which is so important for the defence of Moscow. Bad weather and supply conditions, as well as the poor condition of the troops, in addition to violently and once again offensively fighting opponents, hampered and slowed down the German offensive.

(64) War report to his family, [Likhvin] 5 November 1941 (BA-MA, N 265/155, fol. 127)

Two days ago the weather changed. It is getting colder from day to day. Today it is about 5°C below freezing. The swampy roads freeze and turn into bumpy obstacle courses, which are not exactly beneficial for our cars. Yet by and large our mobility has improved. It was a special event when the first supply train arrived yesterday. …

In this fine weather the city of Likhvin appears in a much more favourable light than before. Not ugly at all, it is located on the steep western bank of the River Oka, about 30 to 40m above the river. Deep clay gorges separate the city at the sides as if it were a castle. From the market place there is a view over the lowland of the Oka, about 4km wide. The air is extremely clear. The entire country looks brownish. Brown is the dominating colour here, including the Russian uniforms. The area around Likhvin is agriculturally wealthy, because the soil is rich clay. But since the peasants have to give away everything, they are poor regardless. Not far away from the city there are coal pits, which seem to have been developed only recently. And a plant for grenades has been set up here. We have captured masses of blanks and 15,000 litres of petrol and oil there. Alas the Russian petrol is useless for our vehicles.

There are a lot of partisans around here. The Bolshevik government has ordered all party members to remain and fight as partisans.[47] They destroy all supplies – in Likhvin they have burnt leather worth eight million marks – and attack, unfortunately not without success in some cases. They mostly attack small requisition commandos, which are sent out by the troops to get hold of food. During the day they hide in the forest and in gorges, at night they get food from the villages. Our Russian interpreter has made it his business to fight them vigorously. The people here often denunciate partisans, because they fear the oppression by them. We can only get them with the peasants' help. Our interpreter was able to catch and kill fifteen in the last three days, among them several women. They are a committed gang. They get shot without revealing their comrades. They know that they will be exterminated without mercy. And yet they say nothing and claim to know nothing. They have actual hamster stashes. In one of them our men found 3 centner [150kg] of honey the day before yesterday, not to mention clothes, meat and flour supplies. Apart from partisans, there are several Red Army soldiers in the area, who remained here after the battles and who roved around, some armed, some unarmed, many of them supporting the partisans.

After the weather has become better and more advantageous for our mobility, we hope to continue our advance on Moscow. The wet period has given the Russian two weeks to bring in troops and to improve his situation. Thus we have to expect significant battles.

(65) Letter to his wife, [Likhvin] 6 November 1941 (BA-MA, N 265/155, fol. 128)

Yesterday I went back to the fox farm. Again, soldiers had stolen six of the largest foxes. Besides, it is said that Hermann Göring has confiscated all noble furs of animal farms. That means we can kiss goodbye the blue fox for you.

Christmas – leave – a big question mark?! It does *not* look like it, at the moment. Transport facilities to Germany are lousy and secondly nobody knows how the war situation will develop. For now there is no end in sight to the fighting. And we are right at a spot where we will be indispensable in the future, because we have to approach Moscow to the southeast. We have probably the most unpleasant tasks ahead of us.

(66) Diary entry, [Likhvin] 6 November 1941 (BA-MA, N 265/11)

Partisan actions at Likhvin are increasing. On 6 November Beutelsbacher catches sixty, among them forty Red Army soldiers; he convicts and finishes off twenty of them. One young man was hanged in the city centre, or more precisely he relieved the military policemen from this unpleasant work and did it himself. Balzen watched this incident with interest. This war is getting nastier and nastier. Everybody is impressed by the partisans' steadfastness. They all remain silent, do not reveal anything and die.

(67) Diary entry, [Grjasnovo][48] 7 November 1941 (BA-MA, N 265/11)

I tell Beutelsbacher not to hang the partisans closer than 100m to my window. Not a pleasant view in the morning. Moy[49] said that Goethe, when he lived in Jena, had a view on a gallows for three weeks.

(68) Letter to his wife, [Grjasnovo] 8 November 1941 (BA-MA, N 265/155, fos. 129f.)

Again, there are new combat actions ahead of us, after the last two weeks have been rather quiet. The weather stays bad, around zero; there is snow and freezing temperatures at night, fog and rain during the day. The roads are either so slippery that our cars spin like humming tops or they turn into a deep swamp. At the moment we live in a miserable village, our quarters are terribly bug-infested. Our men keep asking me, when will this finally end? I can only shrug and answer: I do not know. Others ask when there will be the next leave, but one cannot help smiling. …

Many men have caught a cold due to the miserable weather and the itch is getting more and more common due to the lice-ridden environment. For weeks it has been impossible to have a bath. Clothing and boots of the troops are overused and nearly fall apart. The Russians are better dressed than we are. But the main thing is that they will lose the war anyway.

(69) Letter to his wife, [Grjasnovo] 15 November 1941 (BA-MA, N 265/155, fol. 131)

Some rough days are behind us and they are still not over yet. Our new army, led by Guderian . . ., has forced us – despite our objections – into an operation which initially was pretty successful, but tailed off due to the lack of forces and support from our neighbouring units – just as we predicted – and changed to the contrary making us pay heavy losses. In four days we lost 1,000 men, 790 dead or injured, 180 frozen to death. We had temperatures of minus 20°C for several days, freezing gales stinging like needles. Now it is 'warm' with minus 8 to minus 10°, but always windy. To fight in such conditions, to lie on the ground for hours, facing enemy fire, without the possibility to dig oneself in, is almost beyond human endurance. But that's how it is here.

My fur clothes have not arrived yet. I was told that they are stuck on the road behind Kaluga. I can only hope that they will arrive sometime in the foreseeable future. For the time being, I wear a couple of layers of woollen cloths.

(70) War report to his family, [Grjasnovo] 19 November 1941 (BA-MA, N 265/155, fos. 132–5)

Minus 10°, minus 15°, minus 19°C. That's the temperatures in which we have to work and fight from 8 November. They fluctuate between those figures. The change of temperature is hardly noticeable, but what does make a difference is the wind. Sometimes it is completely windless, sometimes a freezing northerly or northeasterly wind blows which makes it almost unbearable to be outside. It stings like needles in the face and blows through headgear and gloves. And it was under these very conditions, when it was 20°C below freezing and this wind blew, that our men had to lie on the frozen ground for hours while they were under grenade and machine gun fire for two long days, standing out against the light blanket of snow just like the partridges in France last year. One half of them have got headgear and gloves and they all wear only our German coats and thin old trousers.[50] Opposite was the Russian in quilted uniforms, coats and trousers, which look like duvets, with round warm fur earflap caps. These were outrageous combat conditions. And then, on top of that, were the difficulties of supply from the beginning of the month, which took now full effect. For eight to ten days we had neither tea nor coffee, nor cigarettes and cigars, let alone alcohol, often no bread. Ammunition was running low so that we sometimes did not have enough to shoot. It is almost a miracle that we had only 180 men with frostbite who had to go to the field hospital.

The Russian has used the time very well, while we were forced to stand still or could only move at a snail's pace. Whatever troops he could gather he has positioned around Moscow. While we had almost no enemy before us at all at the end of October – and if he did show up, he retreated – we faced a not yet fortified, but occupied position on 10 November. Against our advice and will, we were ordered to engage with the enemy, although we did not have any neighbours on the left or the right, and those who were beyond these gaps were not prepared to support us. Since conducting an attack across a snowy terrain is extremely difficult and involves heavy losses, we broke into the position at night. The Russian was in the villages; he had left the hills due to the freezing cold. That way we forged ahead, sometimes without meeting any resistance, for up to 15km in one go. Yet in the villages the enemy defended himself surprisingly vigorously. We were engaged in tough close combat. In some places it was midday when they were over. Once we had broken through in the centre, there was no enemy before us and we would have been able to march on without a further shot. But then the Russian attacked our flanks. And since there was no one to give us cover, no one far or wide to join our operation, we could not use our victory. After five days and with violent effort, we could ward off the counterattack in our wide bridgehead-like position. We have taken 2,000 prisoners, guns, six tanks and masses of other materiel. But the great victory we had gained was in vain in terms of its operational effect. We ourselves lost 800 heads. Given current force levels, these losses are hardly affordable.

As here, the Russian defends the crucially important area around Moscow everywhere with counterattacks here and there by strong units and tanks. On the other hand we have gained a breakthrough in some places. One of them fortunately jeopardizes Moscow's water supply. Yet overall we are too far away from the city at the moment, so that its fall cannot be expected soon. The advance on the city will be at the cost of heavy battles, because the enemy is reinforcing his troops all the time. The first divisions of the Russian Far East Army have arrived here now. I do not know if the Russians assume that the Japanese will not get involved in the war after all or if they have substituted these troops with new units during the last months. They had plenty of time to do so. Now we can only hope that we will not have lots of snow. If that does happen our difficulties will grow immensely, particularly for our vaunted motorized troops. They have the same difficulties in terms of supplies and mobility. Only the infantry and the panje carriages are able to move here.

Our quarters are in a small village; they are modest and overcrowded, next to a completely destroyed church with a dead frozen horse lying in there. There are masses of well-fed grey mice in the fields scurrying from hole to hole. Often we have steel blue skies and cold sunshine, often beautiful rime. We often enjoy peculiar and particularly colourful sunsets. But the most beautiful thing is the starry sky above us in all its undreamt and pure beauty. The stars flicker and twinkle like brilliants on black velvet. This dry cold is per se a healthy climate when wrapped up warm enough. Compared with Germany in November this weather is to recommend: November in Moscow, that is glorious sun, snow, calm cold. Good place for ice skating and sledging, skiing conditions are improving. Not many conveniences, but low prices. Sauna in every village! Bugs, lice, mice and rats in every house without fail. Blood type 0 preferred by bugs!

There are huge forests very close by. A stream of Red Army soldiers, who have remained behind in the wake of the battle of Vyazma and Bryansk, continuously rush across them towards Tula to get back to their front. In small groups of three to five men they walk along the train tracks avoiding the main roads. Usually they evade when we find them and fight only in self-defence. A division commander with 400 men, Mr Alexandroff, passed our quarters at a distance of only 2km and not one of us noticed them in time. Very often these Red Army soldiers wear ragged peasants' clothes, sometimes with their uniforms underneath. They have grown beards, because they have learned that the Germans do not touch the elderly. Sewn in their furs, especially their hats and their quilted trousers, they keep slips of paper with signs used by criminals, which no one can decipher. Apart from them there are partisans up to mischief. Time and again they attack single cars or people whom they usually kill; they blow up rail tracks and cut telephone cables. We can only get these partisans with the help of the Russian people living here. They are happy to share information, because they themselves are terrorized and robbed of their food by these brigands, etc. We are constantly fighting against this pest. But it is difficult to finish it because the terrain is too endlessly vast, the forest too huge and the hiding places too many. Our interpreter, Lieutenant Beutelsbacher, who is himself from Odessa in the Ukraine, whose father was killed and his brother liquidated by the Bolsheviks, whose mother and sisters were sent to Siberia and made forced labourers in road construction works, fights vigorously against these partisans. Time and again he sets out together with some military police officers and supported by three devoted Red Army soldiers (sons of peasants). He never comes back without having shot dead or hanged several brigands. Almost always these people endure death with stoicism. They do not reveal any names and never testify. They only answer when they are found guilty after having been grilled for hours: I did it by command. An eighteen-year-old guy, who identified himself as the leader of the partisan cavalry unit, tied the knot himself and cried: 'I die for Communism!' and jumped into it. My orderly, who went to see the execution in the market place, said: 'He sought death.' Such fanatical fighters for communism are legion. Time and again one can see them hanging in the villages, but even more are still around. When I ordered them to bury those partisans hanged within sight of our prospective quarters because the sight is, although common, not pleasant in front of our windows, the village people pulled off the hanged persons' boots and furs and pulled the dead with strings to their graves. That's how it looks here. It is like the Thirty Years War, the same habits and customs. Only those who have power have any rights. I have been involved in war for six and a half years, but I have never experienced anything like this.

Our supply transports are still very poor. Under normal circumstances there is a train for the corps every second day. We have had two within four weeks. That means that we have to live entirely from the land. That has been possible until now in regard to meat and flour, even though the men had to bake their own bread. There are no vegetables and fruit except for white cabbage, which is now frozen. Potatoes are already getting short. Sometimes they are stuck in the frozen soil. Soon the region where we are stationed will be completely emptied. When the situation worsened the other day, I arranged for the division to be supplied by aeroplanes which dropped boxes of food by parachute. In this situation we got hold of a newspaper – even though an old one – in which a war correspondent wrote: 'The advance is going so swiftly that headquarters cannot follow the troops.

Supply transports go like clockwork regardless.' Our clock seems to have broken weeks ago though.

(71) Letter to his wife, [Grjasnovo] 19 November 1941 (BA-MA, N 265/155, fos. 136f.)

The day before yesterday the fur clothing arrived, also padded gloves from the army clothing office. The one scarf was among the clothes. I am amply equipped with everything. Please do not send any more warm clothing, except woollen underpants and two or three woollen socks. You *should* have the woollen underpants; you have probably just forgotten to put them in the parcel. Buy the socks. I attach my clothing ration card. Do not waste it. You never know if we may need it some time. Maybe to buy lining material for the French suits in case I do get leave.

Yet I am quite sceptical about that. For the time being no one really knows if the war goes on or if there will be a break. I doubt that we will reach Moscow this winter. If it starts snowing – and it does look like it tonight – then we will be stuck here.

If the fighting goes on, leave will be impossible. Then there will not be a break before December and then we will be busy preparing the next positional warfare. It is another question how to get home in this wintery weather. Aeroplane – blizzard? Car – snow drifts? Train? You can see from the attached report about that. You had better expect a Christmas without me. I am sorry that I cannot say anything else. I wish it could be different. Everyone is sick of this here and would love to go home on leave since there is no end in sight. It will be going on, even for next year. Russia is crumbling, but not yet beaten . . .

I suggest you file my war reports, because I would like to keep them in memory of the war. You always got the best copies and it would be a shame if they got lost after being carried around for weeks in your purse.

(72) Diary entry, [Grjasnovo] 21 November 1941 (BA-MA, N 265/11)

When arriving at Grjasnovo we witnessed the end of a commissar, who tried to escape, at the hands of our military police. Not a pleasant sight for our men.

(73) Diary entry, [Grjasnovo] 23 November 1941 (BA-MA, N 265/11)

After the meeting, a memorial ceremony for our fallen since it is *Totensonntag* [the last Sunday before Advent, on which the dead are commemorated]. ... Then a walk to the 'dead Russian'. This is an extraordinary destination for a walk: a dead Russian has been lying there for weeks in the snow unburied and frozen. I have to ask the village people to bury him.[51]

(74) Letter to his wife, [Grjasnovo] 25 November 1941 (BA-MA, N 265/155, fos. 139–41)

Colonel-General von Kleist's son,[52] a pilot, who is relocated to Antwerp after having been here, will take this letter back to Germany. Only pilots and people like them are that lucky, we are not. ...

After we have been waiting and doing more or less nothing since 15 November, the fighting has started again. I hope it will be easier than the former battles. But we cannot expect anything else ... given the doggedness of the Russians. ...

It is constantly cold, light snowfall since yesterday. Thus it is a bit milder now, but only since tonight. This morning it was again minus 14°C. I often wear these Russian felt boots. That way, at least my feet stay warm. In this respect the boots are excellent. There is nothing else to tell. I am quite busy preparing our offensives. They are difficult to conduct because we have no neighbours to speak of who could support us and there will be danger from both sides, which is not easy to cope with.

* * *

Between 27 and 29 November the corps finally succeeded in breaking through the Soviet defence lines at Aleksin and conquering the city. In the wake of this last important victory before the Red Army's counterattack, the offensive potential of the XXXXIII Army Corps was exhausted for good. Its two substantially worn divisions (the 31st and 131st Infantry Divisions) had to fend off the first Soviet counterattacks from 1 December onwards.

(75) War report to his family, [Grjasnovo] 29 November 1941 (BA-MA, N 265/155, fol. 142)

Three days of heavy fighting lie behind us. We had the chance to lever out a cornerstone of the Russian defence forces south of Moscow, the position at Aleksin. On the first day we had the heaviest battles. On the second, when the outcome was still undecided, our aeroplanes reported a Russian column 15km long advancing on our flanks. The extremely weakened regiments had to face this advance in the forest where defending themselves was difficult. It was a moment of utmost tension. Temporarily we stopped the offensive. We were close to going back to our initial position. Two different aeroplanes reported the same. One hour later these reports proved false. We continued the attack and broke through. Now the entire Russian Front at Tula is jeopardized. The Russian fights with utmost doggedness. His artillery has caused us heavy losses in some places. He has surrounded himself with a belt of mines. He has got new ones; they look like a box some 20cm in length, 5cm in height and in width, made out of thin wood. They only have to be placed in the snow. They have caused a lot of damage. But the worst for the infantry was again to lie on the bare ground for hours, without protection, under enemy fire. The ground is frozen one metre deep. Without being able to move, the men had to remain in the same spot for ten hours. Three of them just froze to death. Besides, all villages are destroyed; the remaining houses shot to pieces, ruined. Tonight a battalion has to sleep in four sheds, the horses have to stay outside, supplies do not come through; it is beyond belief what the men accomplish here.

(76) Diary entry, [Grjasnovo] 30 November 1941 (BA-MA, N 265/11)

Russians and Germans in their winter uniforms are hardly distinguishable. The Germans wear Russian fur hats.

(77) Letter to his wife, [Grjasnovo] 1 December 1941 (BA-MA, N 265/12, fol. 131)

We are in dire straits right now. The enemy vigorously attacks our newly won positions. Our men are extremely exhausted. And we have around minus 20°C and a freezing wind from the north which blows the snow like clouds across the ground. The situation is as bad as never before and we dread the most unpleasant consequences. The situation is especially threatening because our troops are at the end of their tether. ...

Kluge has achieved considerable successes at the North Front at Moscow. South of the city of Tula and where we are Guderian tries the same and more but with insufficient means. We are the ones to suffer. We know only one thing: it cannot go on like this on a permanent basis. The losses are very high; the strain on the men is beyond the power of human endurance.

(78) Diary entry, [Grjasnovo] 4 December 1941 (BA-MA, N 265/11)

Our position in front of the forest which was ideal during the summer is terrible in winter because there is no shelter. Positional infantry and artillery are located in the front-line villages with their most necessary vehicles and limbers. Here it is overcrowded everywhere. Thirty people are happy to have one room. They cannot lie down, but stand just to be in a warm place. It is impossible to wash. There are lice everywhere, we incessantly scratch and scrape. Many men suffer from bladder and bowel diseases due to the cold floor they have to lie on and they do not get a good rest because they wake up many times during the night. It is impossible to accommodate the reserves so that they can be ready to step in immediately. One gets used to that – always hoping that if the Russian does break through, he will not penetrate deeply into our lines. In this war all tactical rules are messed up. Now it is common to fight at a combat width which was previously considered unreasonable. It is common to hold positions covering many kilometres with companies of only forty men, but all these men at the front line are so stressed and strained due to these conditions that it all draws to a close. There are three main complaints I am confronted with: Why did the 2nd Panzer Army order us to attack without being sure that they could come to support us? Now our blood sacrifices, which are hardly bearable given our limited strength (635 heads of the 131st Division from 27 November, including the sick), are in vain. Why do our troops get jam instead of fat although fat is a necessity in this cold weather? Why do they send us out to fight a winter war with insufficient clothing and to face challenges that are beyond human strength? Does anybody know what's going on here? ...

[On 3 December] I went to see Drescher's regiment.[53] The Russian Do-Gerät[54] was rolling in volley fire, our own and enemy artillery was banging away, there was one attack after another, the regiment commander welcomed me almost in tears. Yesterday a company ran away. He lined them all up afterwards and asked them, 'How can you do such a thing?', whereupon the men started to cry. 'We cannot go on any longer, Colonel!' The rest of his regiment is melting away. Drescher says if he loses these remaining men he will not be able to build up the regiment. Companies of just nineteen or twenty men, it is impossible to fight with. And the Russian throws in more and more people.

And again the plea, the request, the cry for sufficient food supplies; first and foremost fat, for appropriate clothing and even more for replacements to fill up our lines. Colonel Drescher says: 'Our men are in such a state that I cannot rule out that one person might point his gun against his own officer because he is truly desperate and loses his head.' Three cases of self-mutilation happened during the last days, all involving men with impeccable records. ...

At midday [on 3 December] Colonel-General Guderian came accompanied by two armoured scout cars in misty weather and driving snow. After a quick lunch I described the troops' condition: the 131st Division extremely exhausted, not able to attack or to fend off heavy attacks. The 31st Division able to conduct a limited attack. ... I reported the increasing number of sick people due to a poor, entirely fat-free diet and completely insufficient winter clothing; I described the poor supply and transport situation. Between two armies and without any motorized vehicles – because they are all broken except for the occasional one – we have to travel for many days just to get necessary things to our position. Very often we do not get any provisions at all for half a week. We have got used to it now and help ourselves. But the area where we have been deployed for six weeks is empty and there is nothing more to find. I tell him that it cannot go on like this if we do not get at least fat and reasonably useful winter clothing this instant, and proper and regular provisions in future. Because right now we are getting *shortened* provisions for two days and then nothing for several days. ... The General replied that he had heard similar things elsewhere. Yet he admitted that *our* provisions were the worst because no other corps had to fight under supply conditions as bad as ours. Other units also had better clothing than us, because the uniforms we were entitled to were sent to the 2nd Army, which we left after being assigned to the Panzer Army. But units were depleted everywhere at a catastrophic level and the fighting morale of the divisions was lowered extremely. Therefore he flew to the army group and asked for orders, but his request was not met with understanding and approval. He also failed to convince even higher authorities to give the order to cancel the operation. The Commander-in-Chief of the Army ordered him to reach a line, which is impossible to hold in the long run (I think Mikhaylov–Skopin was mentioned). Finally Field Marshal von Bock gave the following order: 'Forward without delay and take Tula.' Accordingly he ordered the last attack, which started on 1 December by the 24th Panzer Corps. ...

When I picked Guderian up for dinner at 8.00pm, he had just received news about the state of affairs of the 24th Panzer Corps. East of Tula the advance is going slowly, but it is moving. North of Tula the 4th Panzer Division with battle group Eberbach has reached the main road at Kostrova. The Panzer division itself is at the railway station at Revjakino. The enemy is pressing them hard from the north. Eberbach has thirty tanks, which is not exactly a powerful force. We must expect that he will be attacked tomorrow as well. Thus Guderian's first question for me was: Could you start your attack already on the 5th instead on 6 December? I answered: 'Given the current situation and the latest developments we have to try to be ready on 5 December. Since both regiments know their sections, it might be possible. After having consulted the division I will set the earliest possible date.' . . .

It has been getting cold. At 9.00pm [on 4 December] a pilot told us temperatures of minus 30°C are forecast for tomorrow. We did not expect that. None of us was aware of the impact of this weather change. I told my officers not to give this information to the 31st Division, because it would turn the mood down. And that is undesirable, because we cannot do anything about it anyway. The ball is set rolling.

* * *

According to Colonel-General Guderian's attack order from 4 December the 31st Infantry Division and its two Infantry Regiments (17 and 82) were given the objective to fight their way eastwards to the road between Tula and Moscow and to link up there with the 5th Panzer Brigade under Colonel Heinrich Eberbach, which was supposed to penetrate from the east. Thus the encirclement around the embattled city of Tula would have been closed in the north. Yet the attack, starting in the early hours of 5 December 1941, collapsed swiftly due to increasing frost and Soviet resistance. Consequently all units had to be pulled back to their initial positions during the evening and the night. On the same day, which marked a dramatic turning point in the war, Guderian ordered the operation against Tula to cease. Heinrici describes his visit to Infantry-Regiment 82 in the following diary entry.

(79) Diary entry, [Grjasnovo] 5 December 1941
(BA-MA, N 265/11)

My car is still not ready to go. They say it will take an hour, so I use the time and walk from Merlejevo eastwards to the northern edge of the forest north of Glebovo. I speak to the cannoneers of a battery positioned at the eastern exit of the forest. It is bitterly cold. Instantly the breath freezes on one's headgear. It is very unpleasant to breathe this air. I meet a few men while walking towards the forest who claim the doctor has sent them to the rear area due to frostbite. After 45 minutes I arrive at the Reserve Battalion in a small gorge at the northern edge of the forest. In groups they are standing around small camp fires, frozen; what a pitiful sight. They rub their heels to get warm, but they are completely frozen. I go from fire to fire and speak to them, see their bad situation, tell them to grouch and grouse to let off steam; it sucks here in Russia and there can be nothing worse than this weather. But they do know how close the *rollbahn*[55] is, that it is only a few kilometres to the tanks which have broken through, that after having allied with them Tula will be encircled, and that I am pretty sure this will be the last major attack this winter. The men have had nothing but bread since 8.00pm last night, the coffee is frozen in their canteens. As much as they agree that it is really bad here and nobody is keen on any further advances deep into Russia, they still are somehow in a good mood and I try to cheer up these frozen, poorly clothed, starved, unwashed and dirty people a little bit more. I cannot help thinking that if the Russian saw these people he would not have a lot of respect. That's how pitiful they look. ...

Colonel-General Guderian gives me a call in the evening. I describe the situation, the consequential decision to halt and ask for deploying the 296th Division more to the north. I add that although I do not oversee the overall situation, I would like to point out that the combat strength of the 296th Division is still fresh and intact and that it would not be wise to put it at risk, since after our experiences today they would also freeze to death if they continued their attack. I ask him to take into consideration what will happen when we are stuck on the hills of Kostrova without any protection from the weather.

He answers that he was thinking the same. He has seen the 296th Division himself and has noticed that the men are in a bad condition, not as bad as ours, but still quite remarkable. The XXIV Panzer Corps has expressed the same view as I did. He, Guderian, has therefore decided to cease the operation and to give orders to pull back into the initial positions. This, he said, was the first time that he ordered a retreat. But the circumstances are stronger than the will. He would leave it to me to withdraw either tonight or tomorrow night.

I will choose tomorrow night because I fear that tonight orders will not get through in time, especially to Infantry Regiment 82. But the division asks to start as soon as possible. Without any enemy fire they got to our previous lines in the early hours of 6 December.

About 250 bloody casualties and 850 with frostbite was the result of the day. Infantry Regiment 17 is formed into three reinforced *companies* with ten NCOs, thirty-eight men!! and five heavy machine guns with crew each. With these forces we hold our position!

(80) Diary entry, [Grjasnovo] 6 December
(BA-MA, N 265/11)

I visit the two combat regiments and talk to their commanders. They are in an extremely bitter mood. Colonel Hoßbach,[56] a pessimist par excellence, was even more frustrated because his son had come home with frozen legs. He pours out one accusation after another about the supreme leadership, claiming that it did not recognize the right time to stop.

Again we have minus 30°C, and when I walk up a hill where we will defend ourselves in the section Laderovo–Larino, my fingers almost freeze within five minutes despite fur gloves. There is a dead Russian lying there, half covered by snow, frozen like an ice cube. Terrible country!

What a strange whim of fate that exactly when our men left their quarters to start the attack, the weather turned colder to a degree which even here is uncommon for December. Nobody can fight under these conditions. I could see that for myself when I was out from 6.30am to 5.00pm.

One has to admire the men and what they have accomplished. We were only 9km away from the point where we were supposed to link up with Panzer Brigade Eberbach at Kostrova on the main road. Everyone who has a look on the map will say 'How could this attack be halted?' But we were not able to reach the target on our own after the collapse of Infantry Regiment 17. What we would have lost due to the frost if we had continued the attack is hard to assess. I think we would have arrived without soldiers and would have had to pull out from there immediately. Nature was stronger than human will and ability. Thus the battle of Tula was a failure. I think it could not have turned out differently, because our forces were too weak to fulfil the task from the outset.[57] This does not only apply to our special situation, but to the entire army. Partly due to enemy forces, but partly due to some unfortunate leadership decisions, our weak forces were wasted time and again either by being deployed too far away from each other in the vastness of the country or by being so poorly synchronized that they could not work together. Thus the army was not able to reach the desired success. And it did not help that the strength of the remaining units had dwindled to a ridiculous level and that the men were mentally and physically extremely exhausted after five months of offensive warfare, while the Russian was sending more and more troops against us. Wherever they had come from, they were there, well clothed, well fed, filled up with schnapps and with replacement troops behind them. We have nothing like that. Our victories have brought us to the end of our tether. That is a bitter end. Now we do not even have enough men to watch the position we are supposed to hold.

* * *

On 8 December the XXXXIII Army Corps was attacked by the Soviet 50th Army and gradually pushed back westwards to Kaluga during the following weeks to evade imminent encirclement. Contrary to this was Hitler's unconditional 'Haltebefehl'.[58] *From 19 December the corps was assigned to the 4th Army again.*

(81) Letter to his wife and daughter, [Grjasnovo] 8 December 1941 (BA-MA, N 265/12, fos. 131–3)

With all my heart I wish both of you a lovely Christmas. I do not dare to wish for a merry one. The war presses upon us and the entire German people so heavily. …

I have no idea where we will spend Christmas, but probably not in Grjasnovo, which translates into German as *Dreckdorf* [dirt hole]. For more than four weeks we have been staying here, where everything is cramped and reminds us of unpleasant events. I do not want to spend Christmas here. How we will spend Christmas I have not the slightest idea either. I consider it possible that the Russian tries his best to spoil our Christmas. He will probably assume that he can catch us off-guard on this particular day and will attack. Thus it is likely that our Silent Night will be filled with the rumble of gunfire. … We and the troops would have preferred it if it had been over *before* the winter. In that case we still would have quite intact troops, positions appropriate for fighting, quarters sufficient for the winter. But now we have none of that.

(82) War report to his family, [Grjasnovo] 11 December 1941 (BA-MA, N 265/12, fos. 134–9)

Look at the guys who have been facing the enemy for weeks in this freezing weather. With thirty others they share a lice-ridden panje shed, without soap, unwashed and unshaved for days, with infected wounds all over the body due to constant scratching because of the lice, in ragged uniforms, filthy and covered in bugs. Look at them and hear what they were saying when they were, according to the doctor, unfit for duty due to ulcerous legs. They all declared on 26 November: We are not going into field hospital, we are not leaving our comrades alone right now before the attack. And they came with us the next day in minus 10°C with dressed feet and without socks. And this young lieutenant H. whom I visited with his company, who showed me his men and was found unconscious the next morning. He was wounded three days ago and did not say a word, because he did not want to leave his company, which had lost all its NCOs!

But for all that, we attacked again on 5 December. The situation forced us to do so. The tanks had encircled Tula so that there was only a small gap of 20km at the rear of the enemy lines to close. Our men fought all alone at the Tula–Moscow road, the main transport route for enemy supplies, heavily attacked by our opponent. It would have been a crime not to use and finish this situation, which would have meant a complete encirclement of the Russian. We had been fighting for this very end all along. All our losses and sacrifices have been for the sake of this last step, which had to be taken. It was difficult to reorganize the corps in a minimum of time by combining the strength of all units so that it was sufficient for our objective. Two regiments which were still fresh and not as strained as others by previous combat qualified for that. When we prepared our operation we had driving snow and relatively warm weather with minus 2° or 3°C. But when we started the attack twenty-four hours later at midnight, we had minus 32°C! The left regiment penetrated energetically towards the first target. It was only 8km away from the tanks. The right regiment, however, got stuck in the Russian position. It tried to charge twice during that day and partly succeeded. But most of the regiment was stuck before the villages, entrenched by the Russian, without any protection, in minus 32°C, in the snow. Already at midday, the losses due to frostbite were so huge that the troops just dissolved. A third attack planned at 2.00pm did not happen, because some companies had only a few men left. After gathering all forces including artillery I tried another assault at 4.30pm and failed again. The battalion which was assigned to carry out the attack – a famous one in our army before the war – had crumbled away. Thus by nightfall, I was so close to the desired objective for which we had fought for weeks in heavy battles, close enough to be almost within reach – while the troops supposed to do this had been slipping through my fingers. There was nothing else to do but to suggest cancelling the operation to my superiors. Similar conditions were to be found elsewhere although not quite as bad as ours. Therefore my superiors swiftly made the decision to abandon the operation. So close to our objective and just about to take the last step, we lost what was already in our grasp due to an act of nature. Thank God, by the way, that they made this decision to cancel. We had minus 35°C the next day and minus 22°C the day after that. Had we continued the assault, we would have lost the entire troops in the next forty-eight hours. On the fourth day we had snow drifts which hampered the bringing in of our supplies. By continuing the operation we would not only have frozen, but also starved to death.

I am not sure if my insufficient description of the events can convey the ups and downs of wishes, hopes, resignation, new attacks and successes, and then, finally, failure, which marked these days. It was not a peaceful beginning of advent; rather it was one of the most difficult times of this campaign. Maybe now you understand the full meaning of the Wehrmacht report, which was published twenty-four hours after the events here saying that henceforth the Russian winter dictates the operations. But it takes two to be willing to subordinate to the necessities of winter. I am not sure if they have asked what the Russian thinks of that. For the time being he does not comply with this intention, but attacks us severely at different points. His Siberians have arrived. Used to the cold and well dressed, they seem to consider these temperatures as mild. And that's why he has been pretty successful at some places. What we have experienced on a small scale is also true for different front lines on a large one.[59] At different front lines we were 25km away from Moscow city centre. I doubt that we can and will stay there. We have been thrown out of Rostov.[60] It is all quite dissatisfying at the moment. I have pointed out repeatedly that the Russian is tumbling, but not yet beaten. We have noticed that time and again, experiencing his dogged resistance. With his approaching forces from the far east he can give us a hard time. The Russian will not be beaten until we have defeated him in a new campaign in the summer of 1942. Yet for the time being he seems intent on attacking our exhausted army, already depleted by heavy losses, with all his might during the winter.

All the more we welcome Japan entering the war.[61] I do not expect that it will turn against Russia anytime soon. But it stops – or rather hampers – supply transports from America and England to Russia. And this helps a lot. We have already noticed a decrease in the quantities of enemy air planes, artillery and tanks in the last battles. It will be very difficult for the Russian to rectify these shortages himself. Admittedly, he has dragged off machinery from captured factories. Some of it might have reached its destination, but some of it is just standing around on the rail tracks. Yet winter will be over before the buildings will be finished where these machines can start running. And that is a great advantage for us. I am equally pleased that Rommel[62] can hold the North African Front by and large. For them it is also a relief that Japan has entered the war. If the Italians suffer a defeat here, their position, which is quite fragile anyway, will be severely threatened. A defeat in Libya might even grow into a loss of the whole of Africa. And I can imagine that then someone might conceive the idea to land troops on the shores of Europe via North Africa, Spain, Portugal and maybe via the unoccupied territories of France, when the bad Germans are busy elsewhere. I do hope that Japan's entry into the war will put an end to these thoughts. Our yellow allies have started the war surprisingly and successfully.

At the moment it is snowing and stormy. All roads are almost completely covered in snow. The cold wind freezes you to the bone even through the fur. Earlier I tried my usual walk to the dead Russian, who has been lying there unburied since early November. But I could not get through. We had to cope with huge provisions problems during the last weeks. Often the troops had to go hungry. Tobacco, tea or coffee substitute is rare. Fat, which is what we really need here, never came through. Not everywhere is as bad as here. But we are at a spot that is particularly badly provided due to transport difficulties. There is no main supply route or railway in close range. Trains are often stuck for days in the hinterland due to broken engines or sabotage or explosions. Thus the snow is extremely undesirable for us and will cause us many additional problems. Yesterday I read Stalin's speech from 24 October (October Revolution), which the Russian has dropped as leaflets in the German language. He is hoping that the German army, exhausted after the summer campaign, will succumb to the Russian winter climate, the supply problems and the advance of new

Russian winter troops from Siberia, who participated in the battle of Moscow and are therefore partly depleted, but who are already attacking. It is our task to endure. Thus the wishes for leave cannot be fulfilled. I do not think, by the way, they would be feasible in terms of transport.

On the advice of Earl Moy I read some stories by Tolstoy and Leskov. Tolstoy's villa is close to Tula, where a division headquarters is stationed. His country estate, Tolstoy's farms, is very close to our quarters, they are nothing more than depraved panje sheds.[63] Leskov is one of the best Russian writers. His books impressed me very much. One has to admire Tolstoy's strength and clarity in describing the characters in his books. Thanks to him I have discovered why everything in Russia is so behind the times and so depraved. His short story 'A Landlord's Morning' shows the panje as we see him every day, good-natured, faithful, but without initiative, not willing to start anything of his own accord, even refusing to accept charity if it interrupts the routine he has become fond of. He does not want to listen to suggestions for improvement. Needless to say, you do not get anywhere with people like this. Based on this insight my interpreter suggests: The two German protectorates are set up now.[64] They will become good colonial countries. The rest of Russia should be split up into independent republics. The Soviet government has already prepared for this. Up to Lake Baikal they should be dependent on Germany, beyond that region dependent on Japan. Thus the problem of Russia would be solved.

(83) Letter to his wife, [Grjasnovo] 12 December 1941 (BA-MA, N 265/12, fos. 140f.)

I got stuck in the snow 3km away from our 'dirt hole', where we currently are, and had to return. I gave orders to have fresh horses made ready in order to travel just like old Napoleon with sledges and a new horse team rehitched. This country is beyond all measure in everything: in its vastness, its forests, its climate, its masses of people. We had two outbreaks of typhus due to lice. Everything ugly and unpleasant you will find here. Right now I've got your letters from Münster. They are four weeks old. It would be so nice to be home in our own flat, which is now empty and cold. As we are officially at war with America now,[65] it is impossible to say when we will ever be able to use it again. One has to force oneself to get on if one starts thinking about all that. 1/9th of my life I have spent in actual war, even more in warlike times. Besides the Russian does not even think of having a rest during the winter like we want him to. He attacks across a broad front and is very successful in places exceeding 'local' standards. Thus we do not feel very secure here. Huge areas have to be held with a minimum of forces. Whenever the enemy combines his forces at a certain spot, we are in trouble immediately. Besides we are all physically and mentally exhausted after the six-month campaign. We are not happy at all.

(84) Letter to his wife, [south of Kaluga] 16 December 1941 (BA-MA, N 265/155, fol. 157)

I am writing with the greatest concern about the events here. The Russian penetrated the big gaps in our thin front at several places and forced us to retreat. We experience the same conditions as in 1812, deep snow, almost impassable roads, drifting snow, storms and freezing temperatures. I do not know what will become of it. One can only hope that we will succeed in eventually stopping the enemy. But none of us has the slightest idea how to do it. And our son is in the thick of it. He arrived at the front line almost the very day when things started to turn around. I cannot stop thinking of him. And my own worries have piled up high and there is no way out as far as I can see. Weather, country and natural difficulties across the board make every step that would turn things around impossible. Our supreme leadership thought we could ignore circumstances, which defy human power and control. They will finally break us. During the entire [First] World War I have never experienced a situation like the one we have to endure now. However it will end is in God's hands. These days might be decisive for the further course of the war.

(85) Letter to his wife, [southeast of Kaluga] 17 December 1941 (BA-MA, N 265/155, fol. 158)

Although we have always warned of it, it seems that finally our highest authority has realized the danger at hand. Finally help will be sent. God grant that it happens in time. The situation is devilishly serious, it is even worse, it is stretched to breaking point. No one can predict if things will turn out well. Tomorrow we have to face a serious day full of worries. It would not be that bad if officers and troops were not as exhausted as they are after six month of fighting without rest and under continuous physical and mental strain. To make matters worse, our shrunken units are ridiculously small, our provisions are insufficient and our clothing is in no way appropriate to the Russian winter. I always worry about our boy.

It is 10°C below freezing, we have 30 to 40cm of snow and often snowdrifts, marching difficulties of the worst kind and icy conditions. As a result all vehicles are slipping and skidding all over the place.

(86) Letter to his wife, [southeast of Kaluga] 19 December 1941 (BA-MA, N 265/155, fos. 159f.)

Yesterday, after sometimes very heavy combat, we succeeded in holding up the pressing enemy. Yet that does not change the overall situation, which is still more than serious. Now even the supreme leadership realizes that the fate of the entire campaign is at risk. Before that no one wanted to listen to our warnings. Both on the large and the small scale there have been enough reports about the condition and the weakness of our troops. Irrespective of our lack of winter clothing, insufficient provisions, poor supplies and depleted strength, the Supreme Army Command wanted to advance on Moscow, Guderian on Tula. All precautionary measures were put aside. Now they tell us to sacrifice ourselves to get it right again.

I hope that we finally do succeed by concentrating our forces with the utmost effort. For forty-eight hours the Fuehrer himself has been at work. He will send us all the help he can.[66] We cannot oversee what else is happening. God grant that the weather is not going to hamper or even prevent the supporting measures. Germany is far away and transportation is limited while the enemy is right among his resources.

From today we are no longer part of Guderian's but of Kluge's army. We are pleased about that, because the leadership was not clear and good.

(87) Letter to his wife, [southeast of Kaluga] 19 December 1941 in the evening (BA-MA, N 265/155, fol. 160)

The situation is hotting up. There are changes nearly every hour. What was right a moment ago might be wrong an hour later. Everyone who conceives the situation must know that only a miracle can help us. If God will send us one I do not know. The troops and we have done all that is humanly possible to cope with the situation. But it is beyond our strength to turn the situation without help. We have to face up to these facts.

(88) Letter to his wife, [southeast of Kaluga], 20 December 1941 (BA-MA, N 265/155, fos. 161f.)

It is becoming apparent that we are gradually being surrounded. We are forming a semi-circle southeast of Kaluga and the enemy is encircling our flanks. We do not have any reserves to protect them. All pleas, all requests to our superiors have remained unanswered. Thus we will fall into the Russian's hands either way. Today Brauchitsch resigned as Supreme Commander, Hitler himself has taken over the post. But not even he will be able to turn things around.

I am deeply saddened that Hartmut has to be sent to the front under *these* circumstances. But we have to accept what the dear Lord has decreed. There will be a lot of questions afterwards about the reasons for this surprising turn, which brings ruin on us after we have been at the very top.

We have completely underestimated the Russian. On 3 December the Army Group gave out the message that only one final effort would be needed until the enemy would break down, because he had no replacements left. But he did have his Siberian Army and he did have endless replacements to fill up his weakened units. We, on the other hand, have not had any replacements since the end of June, since October we've had no food and had to live from the country if we could find something, our units have lost their best leaders and troops and are left without proper clothing in the midst of the Russian winter. One has to greatly admire what these overburdened, depleted, lice-ridden and exhausted men have achieved. That's that. Now they will be crushed by the Russian masses. Many hounds soon catch the hare.

* * *

On 21 December the XXXXIII Army Corps finally received permission to pull back to Kaluga in order to secure a way out towards the northwest. The town could be defended until 30 December 1941, afterwards the corps had to retreat towards Yukhnov.

(89) Letter to his wife, [Kaluga] 22 December 1941 (BA-MA, N 265/155, fos. 165f.)

I have the opportunity to send this letter via courier. I have no idea when you will get the *Feldpost* [German military postal service] letters of the last days.

The Russian started his counterattack near Tula on 8 or 9 December. Equipped with phenomenal winter gear, he penetrated the wide gaps in our front. Time and again we were told from above to hold, although we could foresee the looming encirclement. But since we could not hold after being surrounded, we had to evade. Retreat in snow and ice is absolutely the same as in the days of Napoleon. The casualties are similarly high. The apathy of the men increases. The state of the troops cannot be described as anything but extremely poor.

I am again standing at a spot where the Russian presses the most. Basically we are already encircled. Yesterday the situation was without any hope. We were anticipating our end in the encirclement. Then, at the very last minute, Kluge gave permission to evade again. That prolonged our existence a little bit longer. God knows how things will end. We have to put everything in God's hands.

The origin of our '*Haltebefehle*' [orders to hold the line], which show a lack of comprehension of the situation, is probably the highest authority himself. In order to involve Japan in the war and to not let it down, we cannot admit failure. And in order to avoid that, we have to hold the line. That means it will come to a bad end. The consequences for the future will be much worse than withdrawing 200km now. Day after day goes on without a decision, and the enemy benefits from this while our situation worsens.

The ups and downs are hardly bearable any more. For ten days I have seen the catastrophe coming, I have called, I have adjured. I get orders which are impossible to complete. Matters are on a razor's edge. Nothing I do makes my superiors see. The consequences are unforeseeable.

Technically I could have avoided the looming catastrophe for my corps. I should have withdrawn 30km but the AOKs [Army High Command] forbade that. Besides it would have made us leave our poor positions and enter the bare snow. The troops did not want that at all because of their pitiful condition.

It might have been a mistake that I did not make a stand against Kluge and Guderian, against the divisions and my superior [Major General Schulz]. In the end, Guderian – who got us into this isolation due to his fabulous leadership – ordered us to hold the line even though the situation was critical. It was no longer possible to execute this command. We would have been able to get away a good deal further than we actually did had our superiors not hesitated, when retreat was in fact inevitable. Keitel's[67] time has come! It has come overnight. While experiencing all this and thinking about the last years, I have to remember the expression: 'Do not be deceived: God is not mocked!' From the very top one can fall into nothingness.

I do not know how all this will go on. Yesterday, in a completely hopeless situation, I read in the calendar Micah 7:7, 'Therefore I will look unto the Lord; I will wait for the God of my salvation: my God will hear me.' He helped us yesterday, when there was no way out. I can only hand over everything to God. Our might is nothing.

Sleeping, eating, drinking, everything is over. Only our whipped-up nerves keep us awake. But this is beyond our strength, to run for our lives day after day and no hope for a turn around, for improvement.

(90) Letter to his wife, [Kaluga] 22 December 1941 (BA-MA, N 265/155, fol. 167)

Things are unstoppably moving forward. From our superiors we get orders to hold, while the Russian is surrounding us. Yesterday we were almost encircled. Once again we were able to save ourselves. If that is possible a second time, I do not know. My hopes are not high.

I am praying to the dear Lord to help me. Without him I am at my wit's end.

(91) Letter to his wife, [Kaluga] 24 December 1941 (BA-MA, N 265/155, fol. 168)

We are going to our doom. And the highest authorities in Berlin do not want to see it. Whom the Gods want to ruin they strike with blindness. That's what we witness every day. No one dares to make a decisive step backwards only on grounds of prestige. They do not want to admit that their army before Moscow is already completely encircled. They refuse to accept that the Russian is able to do such a thing. And in their blindness they tumble into the abyss. They do not want to admit failure. And this will end with the loss of their army before Moscow in four weeks' time, and afterwards with the loss of the war.

Day after day we feel that the noose around our neck is tightening. The Fuehrer does not want to believe it. For us, who see the situation, it is gruelling to have been slaughtered piece by piece for two weeks. Sometimes we can take a breath for twenty-four hours. Then there is again a hailstorm of bad news. Every counter-action fails, because the enemy always has the first option and dictates our actions. The situation is gruelling and unbearable.

I have received your Christmas parcels just in time. Thank you for the Christmas presents. Wistfully I have noticed the nice wrappings, etc. Oh, Trudel, it is hard to be tortured like this.

(92) Letter to his wife, [near Kaluga] 25 December 1941 in the evening (BA-MA, N 265/155, fol. 170)

I have often thought of you. In my mind I have spent the day with you.

Here it was rather unpleasant. Our situation is getting more and more difficult. In our section we can always fend off the Russian attacks. But with sledges and skiers he can get around our flanks and is thus superior to our ponderous bunch. The moment we think we have a break, the enemy starts debouching and advancing once again. It is an unbearable situation. Finally we got permission to evade – but much too late. The amount of vehicles, material and artillery guns we will lose in this process due to the snow-covered roads is hardly foreseeable. They get stuck, slide into the ditches and do not get forward at all. During the entire Great War I never experienced a situation like that. We are all very much frustrated. Thank God we are the only ones in such a situation, threatened from all sides, a single unit on our own.

* * *

After the fall of Kaluga and the abandoning of the position at the Oka River in 1941, the XXXIII Army Corps was trapped in a narrow pocket between Kaluga and Yukhnov, threatened with being squeezed from the north, the south and the east and finally also from the west. All requests to withdraw further to the west were denied on the grounds of Hitler's 'Haltebefehl'. It was not until 15 January 1942 that Hitler permitted the withdrawal of the front towards a 'winter position' [Winterstellung] east of Yukhnov. But at the same time he demanded that the 4th Army held this important junction and defended the rollbahn, the fortified transportation route between Roslavl and Yukhnov, at all costs.

(93) Felber's[68] diary, 1 January 1942 (BA-MA, N 67/1, fol. 9)

Been in Kondrova with Heinrici (XXXXIII Army Corps): 'War is lost.'

(94) Letter to his wife, [Polotnjanyj Zavod] 2 January 1942 (BA-MA, N 265/156, fos. 4f.)

The *feldpost* is no longer operating. It is not getting through, *because the enemy has taken over the railway and is threatening the rollbahn.* I hope I will find an opportunity to send you this letter.

I have not written for a whole week. I could not, because my worries were too heavy. My head was not clear enough and I did not feel like writing. And there was no opportunity to write. Our situation has not improved at all. Your letters in the parcels encourage me to write back.

My corps is forming the wing which was encircled by the enemy on 12 December. He is behind us, with strong forces, lunging out. From the front he attacks day and night. For days we have had 20°, 30° even 35°C below freezing. Our troops are in a pitiful state. On top of our heavy losses is the frostbite. How long the men can survive nobody knows. Maybe they will just disintegrate one day. It has come to that!

For weeks we have seen this tragedy coming. Fourteen days ago we requested, demanded that finally a decision was made above and that the army was disengaged from the enemy. Had they listened to us, everything would have gone well. The Russian would not have been in a position to overtake us. But we were given answers such as we were not allowed to simply give up hard-won territories. Now they dread a 'Napoleonic retreat' and speak of fanatical defence and forbid any withdrawal.[69] Which means that we have to face encirclement.

Supporting measures are so meagre and everything is always too little too late. They forced me into positions that were impossible to hold. Yesterday I told the Supreme Commander[70] it would be only days until he was pushed back in the south. He has been sent here as a strong man, now he should tell them what *we* think, in consideration of all circumstances, or declare he would rather take over his corps again. The answer was that everybody has to stay where they are. Keitel always throws his weight around. But things will turn around for them as well. It is so frustrating to know what is coming, what is inevitable, yet anything I say is like talking to a wall. Hence fate will take its course without mercy. It will be the same on a large scale. I no longer fool myself about the whole course of the war.

They make changes to everything here. Corps, armies change their commanders on a daily basis. Some of them fell ill. One after another is leaving. It seems that the dear Lord has ordained me to endure everything.

(95) Letter to his wife, [near Yukhnov] 6 January 1942 (BA-MA, N 265/156, fol. 8)

Once again the last days were full of commotion. Yesterday everything looked pretty awful. Today there is reason to be a bit calmer. But it is still very disappointing. For thirty days things have been going up and down for us. Thirty days of nervous tension. Thirty days of hope, of waiting, and still no sign of a substantial change. It would be all much worse if the troops had not overcome the rigours of the fighting, of the weather, of the supply problems with incredible toughness and bravery. During the summer and autumn we thought we had done incredible things. And yet that was nothing compared to the situation now.

Yesterday the cold with temperatures of minus 30° to 40°C stopped. Now it is snowing and a fierce wind blows which makes the roads hardly passable. Nothing is in our favour; everything has turned against us. We can only move by using sledges. All other vehicles fail or do not operate properly.

(96) Letter to his wife, [near Yukhnov] 11 January 1942 (BA-MA, N 265/156, fos. 10–12)

Everything has come true exactly as I told my superiors. They have declined all suggestions out of fear of the highest authority. If it is Kluge or Kübler (our new army commander), they are all afraid of the highest authority. And he himself leads according to platitudes such as 'no Napoleonic retreat'; he leaves the flanks open and gives the enemy all the time in the world to march around us and to attack from behind. We hope for new divisions. But they are coming so slowly and in such small numbers, it is simply not good enough to get us out. Thus the Russian is going to win his first battle of annihilation against us. However, it is hard to accept this fate when it is so obvious that the reasons for this development are due to the stubbornness of our leaders. There would have been measures to turn things around, if they had decided to disengage three weeks ago, two weeks ago, even five or six days ago. We have made suggestions often enough. But the Supreme High Command refused them all, acted according to the objective not to give up 20 of the conquered 1200km. And yet it is completely irrelevant where in Russia we are. I do think the time will come when they will regret everything. However, this will make no difference for us.

The situation is already unbelievable. The enemy's pressure is noticeable everywhere. We are constricted to a point where we almost suffocate. Although it is 15°C below freezing, we hardly ever have a roof over our heads, the horses never. Our vehicles are no longer in working condition, the sledges get stuck on the overcrowded roads. For four hours I walked through deep snow today, in the dark. The first stirrings of defeat are everywhere. I reckon that tomorrow our main transportation route will be closed. In a few days probably the railway as well. And what then? Fighting without ammunition and without provisions! All the neighbouring commanding generals have suddenly disappeared, fallen ill, etc. Others are transferred to a different assignment and leave swiftly. It seems that I am supposed to stay, at the outermost point, without any chance of getting away.

(97) Letter to his wife, [near Yukhnov] 20 January 1942 (BA-MA, N 265/156, fol. 13)

We are practically encircled here at Yukhnov. If there is no miracle, our fate will take its course soon. All promised supporting measures failed to appear. None of the promises of help have been fulfilled. If they are still coming, it will be 'too late', the phrase that mirrors our entire campaign and the decisions of the Fuehrer. He ordered us to stay here against the advice of all experts. Without necessity he caused this situation.

I have called on God with all my heart so many times. Until now he has not sent any help. Nerve-racking and without mercy our fate takes its course, every day a bit further. But it will not be long now. All things must pass.

* * *

On 20 January 1942 Heinrici was appointed commander of the 4th Army. Now he had to cope with the impossible situation of the 4th Army defending the small stretch along the rollbahn. This 'lifeline' of his army had to be defended not only in the south and the east, but more and more frequently also against forces coming from the north and the west under the command of General Belov, including partisans, airborne troops and guard cavalrymen who had penetrated the front line. In the following weeks the German troops were trapped in a situation that almost resembled a cauldron battle.

(98) Letter to his wife, [Spas Demensk][71] 21 January 1942 (BA-MA, N 265/156, fol. 14)

Yesterday was again a day that drove me to despair. We were going to be caught in a pincer movement by the Russian from the north and the south. All possible counter-actions failed. We expected to find our fate, without mercy, irrevocably.

In this very moment I received a call and was told that I was appointed commander of the 4th Army succeeding General Kübler, who only recently had taken over its command.[72] Unexpectedly I was pulled out of the thick of the battle. It was God's will.

Now I have to carry the burden of enduring the war with this army. No other German army was in such a situation for as long as anyone can remember. The enemy uses all advancing replacements to annihilate this army. If it is possible to prevent that, nobody can tell. I can only pray to the dear God that he will help me here again and will interfere at the last minute. Today He stemmed the enemy advance with temperatures of minus 38°C, yesterday with minus 42°C.

(99) Diary entry, [Spas Demensk] 21 January 1942 (BA-MA, N 265/14, fol. 1)

In the morning I drove to the army. 42° below freezing. *Rollbahn* clear. Dead Russians, broken vehicles lying at the edge of the road, covered with snow. The continuous and extreme cold weather is unusual even here. Met General Kübler. He has lost his command, because he told the Fuehrer that he did not believe it possible to hold the *rollbahn* and Yukhnov with the army. Maybe he will be proved right. But because he did not show unconditional faith and said so, they sent him away. Situation of army is tense. Thank God that we can still hold the *rollbahn*, which is our only transportation route for provisions and supplies.

(100) Diary entry, [Spas Demensk] 27 January 1942 (BA-MA, N 265/14, fol. 8)

This morning bad news: the *rollbahn* was disrupted and the road to Gzhatsk closed by the enemy northwest of Yukhnov. Both two deadly threats. At the *rollbahn* the situation has been getting worse during the day. We were successful in reconquering a village in the north. In the evening both roads were still closed. And the enemy was pressing against the *rollbahn* from the north out of the forest ... In our rear he landed airborne troops. We did not have anyone there and could not send anyone, because all our troops are tied up in fighting at the existing front line. The closed roads mean the end of our provisions. Only two days and the army will start starving to death.

Our forces to win back the roads are extremely meagre and motley. We do everything to increase them. But where do we get them? It is enough to drive one to despair. And Field Marshal Kluge reminds us that the Fuehrer demands we hold the position east of Yukhnov under all circumstances. It is by no means to be given up. And yet we are encircled in this very position. There is no other way to put it. It will depend on tomorrow if we can get free at the *rollbahn*. I fear not.

(101) Diary entry, [Spas Demensk] 28 January 1942 (BA-MA, N 265/14, fol. 9)

It is so hard to have been in the worst position for eight weeks without a break, to try and try and to fail time and again. But failure is inevitable, because the enemy always has the first option. This situation is caused by the orders of the Fuehrer, who holds everything. Rommel was allowed to evade and subsequently achieved victory,[73] but we have to hold and let the enemy dictate our reactions. Often everything inside me rebels against that. However, we all pretend that everything is going to be fine. I do not know what will come of it.

(102) Letter to his wife, [Spas Demensk] 30 January 1942 (BA-MA, N 265/156, fol. 17)

The grave battle goes on. Yesterday we had a difficult day of crisis. Again we did not meet our objective to get more space. Again all our efforts came to nothing. Our corps is in a pocket surrounded by the enemy from all sides. In order to get there I had to take the Storch today, 25m above the Russians. They shot at us but missed. The whole night I could not sleep because worries kept me awake. It is an incredible waste of energy. Only cognac and tobacco keeps me going.

(103) Letter to his wife, [Spas Demensk] 4 February 1942 (BA-MA, N 265/156, fos. 18f.)

I have been in Yukhnov for four days. To get there I had to take a causeway passing the Russian, who was only 400m away. He did not shoot or we did not hear any shots because of the noise of the engine. My second car, which I had swapped for another one by pure chance, had a flat tyre, stopped and came under fire by mortars and machine guns. But thank God no harm was done.

In Yukhnov we were surrounded by the enemy for three days. The road we took to drive into the town was already closed and impassable by the evening. During the first night we had drifting snow and everything was quiet. The next two nights it was 25° below freezing and full moon. Between 6.30 and 5.30pm Russian aeroplanes on and off. Every fifteen minutes we could hear the engines humming and knew: There is another one again. Shortly afterwards we could hear the hissing of the dropping bombs and then a banging sound. Eighty-two were killed in Yukhnov during the first night, not including the injured. Some 200m away a house was entirely wrecked. We were lying in bed in our wooden house and prayed to God to spare our lives. In His goodness He did. There was no bomb closer than 150 to 200m.

* * *

By launching a limited counterattack on 3 February, the 4th Army succeeded in bridging the gap to the 4th Panzer Army in the north and in so doing averted the greatest danger. Its situation, however, remained precarious, because again and again new enemy troops advanced from its back. Heinrici's suggestion to shorten the front line and to withdraw to a new position west of Yukhnov was again declined.

(104) Diary entry, [Spas Demensk] 5 February 1942 (BA-MA, N 265/14, fol. 11)

The Army Group Centre demands that we tie up our troops at the front line, while the enemy withdraws his men and commits them against our flanks. They are afraid to suggest to the Fuehrer a withdrawal of even a few metres. They all know in fact that it is necessary. But very rarely they express their opinion towards the highest authority, only as a last resort. This way I feel like a swimmer thrown in the water with my arms and legs tied up. We could defend ourselves, but the means are taken away from us or are permitted only too late, when everything is almost over. The situation caused by that could not be worse for leaders and troops alike.

New attacks in the snow which should have been avoided, new severe casualties among our ridiculously weak troops are the result. Our divisions? With a strength of four to 6,000 infantrymen, actually not more than a battalion. For our more than 10,000 casualties we have not even 500 replacements. That is the help we were promised at Christmas and now it is February. Men with frostbitten limbs are not allowed to go to hospital, because our numbers are falling too low. On the front hopelessness is spreading. How long will it go on? Until the Russian winter has turned into mud! That will happen in April. Only eight weeks! That is exactly as long as the rearguard campaign took us so far. All hopes rely on the new Supreme High Commander, he will manage. But this very man caused all these problems in the first place because he stubbornly hangs on to his view.

(105) Letter to his wife, [Spas Demensk] 6 February 1942 (BA-MA, N 265/156, fol. 20)

Again some days of ups and downs. Our situation has improved a little, but is still critical. It used to be forlorn. To be in fear all the time demoralizes and wears down. Everyone wishes for an end of this winter. And yet it will take at least until April. It is still very cold. In early February we had blizzards for three days. All roads were covered in snow a metre deep. Now we have clear skies, 20° to 25°C below freezing and an icy wind. There is no change in sight. I cannot think of anything else than military issues. Nothing else is possible. I cannot get myself to think of anything else, my mind is not at peace. We always live with the uncertainty: how will the day and the night pass by? One can only endure all this with faith in God.

(106) Letter to his wife, [Spas Demensk] 9 February 1942 (BA-MA, N 265/156, fol. 21)

I did not have time to write a letter during the last days. I was at the front line with my old corps. Due to the weather we were spared air raids. There was a lot of damage in this area caused by aerial attacks. Our overall situation has not improved as much as we had hoped for. Every day brings new crises and commotions. Yesterday and this morning we had again some situations. With great difficulty we were just about able to solve them. And we cannot expect to be spared from experiencing new difficulties of the worst kind in the near future. Thus we live in a state of constant nerve-racking tension. Always being outnumbered, always reacting on the enemy's actions. His means seem to be unlimited, while we have shortages and problems almost all the time. He brings on masses of men, while our troops are melting away. Unimaginable difficulties are ahead of us. Nothing arrives on time or as promised. Thus every day is a chain of sorrows that I am dreading. I hardly dare to pick up the phone when it is ringing. Very seldom is the news good. Nevertheless it is an achievement that we have persevered that long. I am longing for a break!

(107) Letter to his wife, [Spas Demensk] 12 February 1942 (BA-MA, N 265/156, fol. 23)

Yesterday I met Field Marshal von Kluge. He was in a surprisingly good mood, although he, too, has a lot of problems. But he is further away from the action than we are. The diary entries describe only military facts. They do not mirror the nerve-racking tension of the current situation. And the worst is: given our situation there is no prospect of change any time soon.

(108) Letter to his wife, [Spas Demensk] 16 February 1942 (BA-MA, N 265/156, fol. 24)

At the moment the Russians attack us like wild animals every day and they are as dogged, tough and desperate as they have ever been before.

(109) Diary entry, [Spas Demensk] 16 February 1942 (BA-MA, N 265/14, fos. 19f.)

I called Field Marshal von Kluge and asked him to change his order to the 2nd Panzer Army. He was very indignant about it. The Supreme Army Command has suggested and wished that we should link up at Mosalsk – which has proved utterly unrealistic: on a 1:300,000 scale map it looks like a good idea, yet it by no means takes our real situation into account (being encircled, commanding divisions with regiments of 100 to 200 men who can fend off the fierce enemy attacks only with the utmost possible effort, example: the 31st Division covering 17km of front line faced seventy-three enemy attacks, the 131st Division, covering 11km, fifty-three enemy attacks of more than company strength between 21 January and 16 February; casualties: 530 dead, 1,400 injured, 1,100 frostbitten). Von Kluge has suggested a small solution as a compromise. ... Yet we cannot even achieve his small solution with our forces. He did not like the idea at all to deviate from his own compromise and to let his superiors down. He vented his anger about General von Unruh[74] (Korück) [*Korück, Kommandant Rückwärtiges Armeegebiet*: rear area commander] for not sticking to the arrangements. Yet this was also unfounded. ...

It is a miracle that the army still exists. If the enemy had acted the right way, we would not have survived. He must have thought that we were already on our knees, thought that he could deploy troops to distant spots who would have been available to engage us from behind. He forgot that a bird in the hand is worth two in the bushes. This is the only reason we have survived so far. But it is a reason we cannot control. A Higher Authority interfered here who disposes. Without Him our encirclement would be a fact and we would not be able to do anything about it.

And it is also a miracle that transports on the *rollbahn* are still running today despite the enemy's effort. Even though he takes the roads under fire, vehicle after vehicle passes face to face to his weapons. Many of them are shot to pieces. But the majority comes through. Yet taken as a whole, this is an unbearable situation for an army.

Finally our replacements are coming in. How long did we wait, hope, pray that they would finally, finally arrive. They are completely insufficient, but better than nothing, because our divisions are worn down.

* * *

As early as January 1942 the Soviet offensive had lost its vigour and by mid-February the overall situation on the Eastern Front had largely stabilized. However, the situation of the 4th Army remained critical until the beginning of May, because their weakened troops had to defend the rollbahn forwards and backwards against the attacks of the Red Army.

(110) Letter to his wife, [Spas Demensk] 19 February 1942 (BA-MA, N 265/156, fol. 25)

Under heaviest losses on both sides we have broken out of the threatening encirclement for now. We annihilated the enemy at four places where he wanted to cut us off. After we found out the numbers of the divisions already positioned in our rear by interrogating the prisoners, we felt like the Rider and the Lake Constance.[75] The danger was much greater than I assumed. Now we completely understand why the Russian thought we – that is our army – were on our knees given our numbers and situation. In all probability it was bound to be over with us. It is thanks to God's help and the bravery of our troops that this did not happen. A Wehrmacht report gave account of a recent battle 80km southeast of Vyazma. After seven days of fighting in a forest three and a half encircled Russian divisions were annihilated. For five days the troops held on in the snow without food or a roof over their heads, protected only by a kind of snow castle, until they were depleted by our artillery fire. They say 3,500 men were killed. The place must have looked awful. I will not go there since it is too disgusting. It was similar with the other cauldrons.

But those were just the tips of the small pincer, which we were able to cut off before it could snap shut. The very big one is still looming.

(111) Diary entry, [Rastenburg] 28 February 1942 (BA-MA, N 265/14, fol. 21)

Flight with Ju [52] from Smolensk to Rastenburg[76] at 10am, arrival 1pm. After lunch with the Fuehrer, discussing the situation of individual armies. Our situation: I reported situation at the *rollbahn*, pressure of the enemy from the south and north (airborne brigades).

Danger: our supplies could be cut off in the next hour; request: to give up Yukhnov. Reason: we need reserves, we have to pull out troops. Otherwise the *rollbahn* will get lost in the rear, because it is held only by units that are scratched together. And the *rollbahn* makes or breaks the entire army. He interposes: then we would give up the road Yukhnov–Gzhatsk, which is the only transportation route during the season of mud. – There he is mistaken. This road is a swamp during the wet period. No help at all.

He fights over this concession. Postpones it. It is not before the end of the meeting, when Kluge also supports the request and describes the Yukhnov–Gzhatsk road as impossible that he agrees. Fuehrer says that it is in fact irrelevant if we are 10km east or west of Yukhnov. As the front has been stabilized, he would not argue about a few kilometres. He said that people might have considered him 'stubborn', because he has resolutely rejected any withdrawal until now. This was necessary to stabilize the front. There have been people who thought that our cause was lost. Only by ordering to hold at all costs was it possible to counteract a panic. (Very true, generally speaking, but wrong in our particular case. This mistake caused our continuously critical situation and our heavy casualties.) Fuehrer shows great interest in technical details, responds to technical issues in particular. He reckons that anti-tank defence is superior to tanks so that tanks will cease to exist by 1942. (?) Considers England to be in similar situation as Germany was in summer 1918. Is very optimistic overall.

(112) Letter to his wife, [Jägerhaus near Rastenburg] 28 February 1942 (BA-MA, N 265/156, fol. 28)

For the first time since Whitsun back in Germany, in decent rooms, in orderly circumstances. It is incredible. There's a water closet, a bath tub and flowers on the table. Unbelievable. Now I am waiting for the phone call with you that I have booked.

Everyone here is very optimistic. Alas, our individual situation is more critical. At present we are under a lot of pressure. It is a relief to get away from the ups and downs just for twenty-four hours as I do today. ...

Tomorrow morning I am going back to Russia with the Ju. How much I would prefer to stay in Germany!

(113) Letter to his wife, [Rastenburg] 1 March 1942 (BA-MA, N 265/156, fol. 29)

Since last night I have been waiting for the telephone call with Freiburg. It has not come through. I have to leave in twenty minutes. We probably will not have the chance to talk. I am very cross about that. There are these people from the Foreign Office who continuously block the line. They have come here and probably report home that the Russian winter in Angerburg [today Węgorzewo] is terrible. And I cannot get through because the line is always engaged, although I have booked an urgent official call.

Most of the people here think that we are, by and large, out of the woods with our Russian winter offensive and that we have won a defensive battle that has weakened the enemy substantially. In regard to England, hopes have been built that they are in the same position as we were in autumn 1918 due to the defeats caused by the Japanese. We'll see.

That does not change anything for me though. General Halder[77] told me that no one is under as much pressure as I am. And indeed the Russian is throttling us. If he gets 500m further, it will be our death.

* * *

After Heinrici returned from the Fuehrer's headquarters, the 4th Army was finally given permission to withdraw to the requested position west of Yukhnov and of the Ugra River on 3 March. They held this line until the end of the Soviet attacks in early May 1942.

(114) Letter to his wife, [Spas Demensk] 3 March 1942 (BA-MA, N 265/156, fol. 30)

I came back the day before yesterday and flew to the front line with the Storch immediately. The bottleneck, which allows us to get to the corps via aeroplane, is 4km wide. The enemy is positioned along the road at a distance of 500 to 1,000m and fires at our vehicles with everything he's got. It will be days before we get new replacements to support us in these areas. Even though our highest authority is optimistic regarding the overall situation, our own situation here is still unpleasant and particularly in these days very critical. To be repeatedly on a knife edge is so nerve-racking and depressing that it demoralizes everyone. It is possible to overcome highly dangerous situations like this once or twice. But living with them constantly, not knowing any other situation, that is a heavy burden for everyone. And this burden is difficult, very difficult to carry. We are happy about every day and every night without disaster. But with great tension we see the next one coming. We can only pray to God for help.

For three weeks the winter here has been like in Arosa: strong sunshine during the day without thaw, 25°C below freezing during the night. We hope for a thaw as it will limit the Russian's mobility. Nobody knows when that will be. It might be any time between 15 March and 15 April. And a lot can happen before then.

(115) Letter to his wife, [Spas Demensk] 5 March (BA-MA, N 265/156, fos. 31f.)

Since this morning the Russian has been attacking us along the entire front line, and not only here where we are but on all main front lines. The prisoners we took say that this offensive is supposed to be the decisive battle we all have been fighting for for so long. On a large part of my front sector the enemy could not achieve this objective, because we had just disengaged with the opponent. I had secured permission to withdraw on my visit in East Prussia the other day – it was easier than I thought it would be. I was told that, after the front has come to a standstill in general, it does not really matter if we are 10km further east or west. By withdrawing we have troops available to support other important and weak points at the *rollbahn*. That proved necessary already today. We had quite a lot of critical situations there. They seemed to be dealt with for the time being. But we are only at the beginning of the battle. It will last again two weeks.

Under the circumstances it will bring a lot of commotion and many sorrows. Thank God the Russian is also quite exhausted and in a bad mood after three months of winter offensive. For the first time after many months we had some Russian defectors.

In your letters you say that the people in Berlin are calmer and more confident about the war and that I should not be worried and get worked up about it. Well, let me tell you that there is quite a difference between looking on a 1:1 million map or actually being here, *sharing* the danger and witnessing the exhausted troops who endure temperatures of 20°C below freezing and who experience almost on a daily basis that combat operations fail and can only be set right with a lot of effort. After all, we have been in battle continuously for eight and a half months, for three months in encirclement. Look on the map: the enemy is everywhere around us. While I am writing, Russian aeroplanes are flying above our position, dropping airborne troops in our rear. This has been going on for six weeks. Nobody stops them. We have not the forces to do so. The troops are in a much luckier position, because they have only their own experiences and thus oversee just a small part of the whole thing. They get into great danger for a while, but afterwards it always gets quieter again. Most of the time the men do not even know in what great a danger they are. I, on the other hand, have to endure both: the hardship of the troops and the sorrows caused by the overall situation. That's how it is.[78]

(116) Diary entry, [Spas Demensk] 8 March 1942 (BA-MA, N 265/14, fol. 23)

Kluge visited. Talked about the situation and further intentions. . . . He is in a very good mood, praises the 'thoughtful' leadership of the army and is of the opinion that the situation has improved. It has been worse. But is not pleasant either.

(117) Diary entry, [Spas Demensk] 9 March 1942 (BA-MA, N 265/14, fos. 23f.)

The position of the army is quite peculiar. Like a ribbon it stands on a front section of 130km bent twice in a refraction angle. The only transportation route is under imminent threat by the enemy on a width of 20km. Airborne troops, skiing battalions and masses of partisans are in the army's rear trying to encompass the ribbon from the other side. Fighting is going on everywhere. Enemy aeroplanes are flying every night over our houses and reinforce their army in our rear. We have not the forces to stop them. With difficulties our vehicles secure the villages that are between the enemy and our transportation routes. This is no longer just a little nuisance but a new army composed of airborne officers, of partisans, former prisoners and of commissars from the population. Weapons including artillery guns and ammunition are easily to be found in the area of the battle of Vyazma. Considering all this, one might wonder whether the enemy is going to abandon the offensive next spring. Instead one might reckon that the enemy is thinking: my objective to defeat the German army during the winter failed, but I have wounded it substantially. Now I will not stop but continue so that I will defeat it in summer.

(118) Letter to his wife, [Spas Demensk] 9 March 1942 (BA-MA, N 265/156, fol. 33)

Enemy attacks and cold weather persist. Always the same sight, always the same events. We are still not just fighting, but fighting for our lives. We have become a bit stronger. But that does not change the fact that our battle is difficult, carries great responsibilities and is full of sorrow. I wish the situation would finally ease. I wish these fierce attacks would finally stop. We were completely mistaken about the strength, the ability and the doggedness of the Russians as well as about their organizational skills and the means they have at their disposal.

(119) Diary entry, [Spas Demensk] 12 March 1942 (BA-MA, N 265/14, fos. 26f.)

Flight with Storch along the *rollbahn* northwards to the 31st Division, later to the XIII Army Corps, 52nd and 137th Divisions. Everywhere complaints about strengths being too low, insufficiently trained replacements, incapable NCOs and starving horses. One has to admit: even though the Russian was not able to banish us from his country, he has depleted our army substantially. Good Lord, how the troops have shrunk. The state of our officers and weapons. Under these circumstances every defeat has an impact twice or three times as much. ...

It is difficult to integrate replacements into the existing troops, because they cannot digest the additional forces due to the lack of experienced leaders. Train! Easier said than done. If almost all troops have to be on sentry duty during the night in freezing and stormy weather due to the vastness of the terrain and during the day field fortifications are to be built, then one cannot expect a lot of initiative to train and be trained.

(120) Diary entry, [Spas Demensk] 13 March 1942 (BA-MA, N 265/14, fol. 28)

Visited prisoners' accommodation at midday and was partly appalled. Ordered remedy. We will only harm ourselves with this.

(121) Letter to his wife, [Spas Demensk] 21 March 1942 (BA-MA, N 265/156, fol. 34)

The enemy tries his utmost to encircle and annihilate us before spring. In front of me I have a planner filled with combat operations we have to conduct in order to prevent this. We still do not know what to expect from the enemy. And yet everyone is longing for peace and rest. From tomorrow we will be fighting continuously for nine months.

(122) Diary entry, [Spas Demensk] 22 March 1942 (BA-MA, N 265/14, fol. 29)

Severe Russian attacks against the Ugra River loop lasting for several days have been warded off after heavy fighting. Casualties were high on both sides, 600 men of our troops. The enemy has probably lost even more. One of his tanks broke through the ice on the Ugra and drowned. Fortunately this secured our positions on this river front. It was remarkable how doggedly the Russian fought and never gave in. He overpowered our heavy weapons from his position on the higher-lying river bank, he crossed the frozen river, gathered at a steep slope and suddenly debouched from there. For three days he has been using these tactics at a spot south from here near Shukowka. Unfortunately he is advancing with tanks there. Seven are damaged or destroyed, partly as a result of the attack by an infantry close-combat tank destruction unit (*Panzervernichtungstrupp*). They fought very bravely. The fight is not yet over there.

(123) Letter to his wife, [Spas Demensk] 25 March 1942 (BA-MA, N 256/156, fos. 35f.)

What gives the most reason for concern is the enemy in our rear who has grown into an army.[79] We have not only a front forwards but also backwards, and not enough troops to secure them. In a way we are swimming like a blue tongue of land in the Red Sea and this is getting wilder and stormier every day from behind, as it has been filled up. It is also to be expected that the enemy will form a huge number of new units out of his masses of human resources. Considering our situation as it has emerged in the course of the winter, they will probably mainly fight *us*. But we have not enough troops. I am very concerned about the ratio between our own and the enemy forces and about the condition of our human and materiel resources. One cannot avoid the impression that the situation is not seen this way where G[yldenfeldt] is.[80] This is not a slight problem for us. Because this view will lead to decisions that will cause a difficult situation for us as was the case in the winter.

Finally the winter seems to take its leave even in this country. After we have had temperatures below zero *continuously* from the end of October – except for one day in early March – and how cold it was sometimes, the weather has turned milder. It is not really thawing right now, but temperatures are pretty close to zero sometimes. Yesterday I even saw an ice cover breaking at one point. Today it is snowing again, but this is just another sign for the end of the winter compared to the continuously freezing temperatures we had before. Everyone here is fed up with both the war and the everlasting white around us. The ordinary men have no other wish than 'relief'. But that is impossible for all of us. …

I would love to write a proper letter again. But most of the time I do not have the peace of mind or I am not in the mood, so I cannot bring myself to do so.

(124) Letter to his wife, [Spas Demensk] 30 March 1942 (BA-MA, N 265/156, fol. 37)

We are facing the heaviest Russian attack the enemy has ever brought against us. For four days he has been attacking with masses of troops and is throwing in more and more every day, infantry, artillery, tanks, aeroplanes at night. Our men fight with great devotion. But it is terribly hard for them. And spring is a long time coming. We have had days of sun and blue skies for eight weeks without exception. That means: without wind it is thawing, during the night it is freezing. We really hope that the 'mud' will bring us some relief. But the enemy is attacking day after day without cease. We cannot achieve anything we wanted to. All our attempts are foiled by the enemy. All this is, as a matter of fact, a result of those decisions that led to this situation. Since now we are in such a position that the enemy simply cannot do anything else than act as he does. Nobody knows how long this will last. But everyone fears that there is no sign of an end.

(125) Letter to his wife, [Spas Demensk] 7 April 1942 (BA-MA, N 265/156, fol. 38)

We are under the pressure of continuous Russian attacks at the most dangerous spots on our front. After we were initially successful in fending them off, the enemy – who has constantly thrown masses of new men into the battle – created a very unpleasant and dangerous situation for us. Yesterday we learned about new forces advancing. We have not enough resources to oppose them. Instead of having some peace and quiet, as Gyldenfeldt told you once, a new and very great danger is looming. The Russian is not backing off but stubbornly pursues his objective to break through the lines exactly where we are and annihilate us. Yet he is attacking not only from the front but also from the rear, where he has positioned a second army that is about to wall us in. We feel gloomy about the future and foresee sorrows and troubles and do not know what will come out of it. We hoped that the spring and wet weather would bring us relief. But nothing of the sort is happening. We still have temperatures below freezing in the night, during the day the sun melts the surface and makes it soft. There is no flooding, no ice drift, no season of mud in sight, which could help us. If anything the Russian aeroplanes are coming – just like right now – flying above us and dropping commissars, airborne troops and officers in our rear. No one stops them or is able to stop them.

(126) Letter to his wife, [Spas Demensk] 13 April 1942 (BA-MA, N 265/156, fol. 39)

It is happening. If the enemy succeeds in holding what he has won today the biggest part of our army is cut off. The *rollbahn* is closed at a spot where we cannot open it up again. The enemy has achieved this success today with some thirty tanks. I have no means to fight back due to the extremely tense situation. The enemy advanced with new troops again from far-away Siberia. We had to face him with our poor exhausted men who have been fighting the enemy for four weeks. The crisis started on the day of Gisela's[81] confirmation. A nice success yesterday seemed to have solved it. But today the setback came. The weather – blizzard, heavy fog – made it impossible to deploy the *Luftwaffe* to support us. Now three corps are tied up and cut off. I do not know what will come out of it. We had hoped for the season of mud to affect the enemy as well as us. It came and did not come. And right now, after the enemy has gained his success, it is starting and makes things even more difficult. All things possible are against us. All vehicles sink in the mud, thus one cannot move at all except on the *rollbahn*, which is now closed. At least that is the case with our vehicles. Russian tanks, lorries and tractors get through.

For three and a half months the Russian has fought for this success. For three and a half months he has failed. And in the last, the very last moment before the weather changed, the weather which should have prevented his victory, he is successful. It is probably fate that it happened.

(127) Letter to his wife, [Spas Demensk] 16 April 1942 (BA-MA, N 265/156, fol. 40)

We have been in the greatest distress over the last few days. The enemy succeeded in positioning himself on one of the most important hills along the *rollbahn*. Miraculously we were able to win it back on the 14th. This was only possible through the terrific efforts of the *Luftwaffe*. Because the weather was so bad, the Stukas dropped bombs from 50m above, so that they put themselves in extreme danger from their own detonations. To recapture the hill has cost us one of our best division commanders, General Berthold,[82] who has commanded the XXXXIII Corps for six weeks succeeding me. He fell in combat for a village. I regret that very much, because he was an excellent man, decent, smart and brave.

The enemy attacks continue. Yesterday, today for the whole afternoon until tonight. The Russian advances through the water, through the swamp. He is not bothered, he brings up division after division, sacrifices hundreds and thousands of men and tries by all available means to achieve his objective, to dent our flank. He has not the slightest intention of abandoning the fight during the season of mud. He minds neither wet nor cold. His tanks drive through the snow as well as through the swamp. He wants to demoralize us. It is difficult to endure this, it is an extreme strain for all leaders and for the troops who are dwindling.

(128) Letter to his wife, [Spas Demensk] 20 April 1942 (BA-MA, N 265/156, fol. 41)

Again we are facing a very critical situation. The Russian is continuously attacking two particularly difficult spots on our front by day and by night. This has been going on for more than two weeks. If a thousand men fall or are injured, the enemy just brings up replacement troops or fresh divisions and goes on attacking us. Watching this people-grinder day and night without ceasing is bound to make one nervous. Ten times we might fend off these attacks, but at the eleventh or twelfth time the Russian is finally successful and penetrates further into our lines. In the end one does not know where to get troops to replace our terribly high number of casualties. We had set our hopes on spring. Now it has been thawing for a couple of days, but we have not felt an improvement yet. For the time being everything is as usual without changes, be it in the snow or in this incredible mud, in which every vehicle bogs down. It is impossible to get out of the village by car where we have taken up our quarters. We have to take a *draisine* and drive 20km over land until we reach the causeway. And here the enemy is only 1,000m away and fires at everything that moves.

(129) Letter to his wife, [Spas Demensk] 21 April 1942 (BA-MA, N 265/156, fol. 43)

Finally spring has come, which means that the snow has been melting away for the last three days. Oddly there has been not a drop of rain. The bright sunshine melted away the snow. At midday it gets as warm as 25°C in sheltered areas. At night temperatures sink below freezing. But just imagine: apart from a light drizzle on 25 March in the afternoon, there has not been a drop of water from above unless it was snow! A strange country. At the moment we are bogged down in mud. There is no way of driving a vehicle.

Last night I was woken up by machine gun fire. 1,000m away from my house, partisans tried to cut a cable. Previously the snow had hampered their activities. Now they come through everywhere. The other day I stayed in Smolensk overnight and witnessed heavy air raids lasting for two hours. And recently a heavy shell landed very close to my car. All these events were not dangerous at all, but we are quite concerned about the future. Every day it becomes more evident that the enemy is preparing for a big strike against the deep flank of my army in order to accomplish the encirclement of Kluge's army. I have warded off a major offensive against my army in the south and the east that has been ongoing since March. The attacks never ceased, as you know. The big strike will probably hit us on 1 May. We warned our superiors and finally we were heard. This is quite an inconvenience for them, but we cannot help it. The fact of the matter is that the enemy dictates our actions here in Russia at the moment.

(130) Letter to his wife, [Spas Demensk] 25 April 1942 (BA-MA, N 265/156, fos. 45f.)

One week of continuous, heavy fighting is behind us. It is relatively quiet on the entire Eastern Front, only where we are the big battle continues despite mud, despite water, despite immobility. The army is in such a devilish situation that the Russian simply has to attack. He is deploying division after division, tank after tank, more and more artillery weapons against us. While I am writing here at 10.30pm, I can hear three to four severe hits for every line I write. And we are always threatened by the possibility that even a marginal loss of terrain, of merely 100m, would lead to the close-down of our famous *rollbahn*. Elsewhere it is about kilometres, here it is about centimetres. Yet behind all these immediate events there is the great offensive. We can watch the preparations, but we have not enough forces to stop them.

But it is aimed directly against me and is supposed to encircle me, and this time for real. Finally our superiors seem to realize what is going on here. General Blumentritt[83] from the Supreme High Command of the Army was here for three days. He used to command an army himself, a very clear-headed, reasonable man who perceived the situation here as it really is: that our troops, like a string of beads, face two fronts so that they can move neither forward nor back, that we have no reserves to make up for a failure, let alone to take action against the enemy on our own initiative. We cannot do anything other than concentrate on these spots in danger, well aware that in so doing new gaps will emerge at different points. Some people wittily suggested putting up signs in Russian along our so-called position saying: No trespassing! Because we do not have any soldiers. Gradually our troops are getting pulverized if they happen to have survived these battles. The commanders tell me that in three weeks I will report: zero soldiers. That is how it looks here.

Yet the highest authority in Germany still hopes that it will go well, after we have been generally lucky for the last four months. And yet artillery fire has become so severe, it will not cease for a minute. My house is shaking and the windows are rattling. Furthermore, our *rollbahn* has broken down due to the wet surface. On a length of 102km, the causeway has turned into a swamp. Three days ago it had to be closed for all traffic. Nothing gets through, lorries and horse carriages are bogging down up to the wheels in mud. All adversities and problems imaginable seem to have conspired against us!

(131) Letter to his wife, [Spas Demensk] 28 April 1942 (BA-MA, N 265/156, fol. 47)

It was a really bad day today. Our important attack went completely wrong. Everything was prepared as precisely as possible. Still it was a failure, a complete failure: heavy casualties, no success at all.[84] The troops are completely run down.

Two days ago Russian bombers were attacking us during the night. No casualties. Today everything deep in snow.

(132) War report to his family, [Spas Demensky] 8 May 1942 (BA-MA, N 265/156, fos. 1–3)

Thousands of prisoners, Russian inhabitants, construction troops are trying to hold the *rollbahn* by setting up boardwalks. But it is nothing more than patchwork. ... Due to the wet period, maybe also due to a major German offensive to be expected, the Russian attacks have ceased during the last days, for the first time since 11 December. For six months there was one attack after another against our lines without ceasing. Again and again, like the waves of the sea against the shore, the Russians were storming against our positions. The battlefields are covered with bodies. In order to compensate for casualties, the Russian brought in new replacement troops all the time to fill up his dwindling units. They were thrown into the front lines as soon as they had been brought up. And if they were gunned down, new divisions came to replace them. It went on and on. But winter, always considered the Russian's ally, has proven itself his opponent at times in some respects. It costs heavy casualties and severe bloodshed to advance against machine guns – as long as they are working – while walking through the snow up to the knee or even up to the belly. We have experienced that ourselves when the circumstances forced us to attack. Two things helped us to hold our position during the winter: our artillery and our superiority in the air. . . . Our depleted infantry only survived thanks to their support. Otherwise we would not have been able to make it. But this winter was an incredible trial for all who were there. Only very few troops are left who started with us on 22 June. But this campaign also had an impact on the higher ranks. Many of them, like me, have been part of it from the beginning until now, have experienced this continuous battle without ceasing, without relief, without leave, without rest. There was nothing like that in the Great War. And back then we were not put in the difficult and critical situations that are almost common now. It is a miracle that we have mastered them every time. Once it is known under what circumstances we did that, how weak our troops were, how great our problems, then people will be wondering how these achievements were even possible. We are no longer surprised by anything.

(133) Letter to his wife, [Spas Demensk] 12 May 1942 (BA-MA, N 265/156, fol. 48)

I feel miserable and exhausted. I am supposed to go on leave at the beginning of June, around the 10th.[85] I would love to go right now. I am at the end of my tether, so discontented and frustrated, shattered, demoralized and worn out by the imbalance between expectations from above and the reality of war. I do not exercise, I smoke too much and ruin myself physically. Everything here is awful.

Chapter 8

Notes to Part II

Note: The following biographies focus on the first year of the eastern war. Information for Hitler and other well-known personalities (e.g. Napoleon, Goethe) is not included.

Chapter 7: General Heinrici – in his own words

1. Lieutenant-General Karl Hollidt (1891–1985), from May to October 1940 Chief of the General Staff of the 9th Army, of which Heinrici's corps was a part.
2. On 12 September 1940 Army Group B (Field Marshal von Bock) with the 4th and 12th Armies was moved to the eastern border to link up with the 18th Army, which previously had been the only unit responsible for border security. *See also DRZW*, vol. 4, pp. 216–19.
3. On the then still unstable German–Romanian relations before Antonescu seized power in September 1940, *see* Hillgruber: *Hitler*, pp. 9–93.
4. *See also* Halder: *Kriegstagebuch*, vol. 1, p. 38 (28 August 1939), on a respective remark by Hitler.
5. Wilhelm Knüppel (born in 1902), Major i.G., since April 1940 first General Staff officer (Ia) of the XXXXIII Army Corps.
6. In hindsight, Heinrici emphasized his scepticism in a much stronger fashion than he did in this diary entry. He then also failed to mention the 'substantial reasons' in favour of the 'eastern campaign'. Heinrici's diary entry, 23 January 1943, in: BA-MA, N 265/13: 'That is for sure, although I always was the only one with this opinion: the war against Russia was not the right one. If his armament and his secret intentions were considered a threat, the art of diplomacy and politics should have averted this danger instead of adding a new, uber-strong enemy to the already existing enemies. In February 1941 I wrote to Otto Kogler who had asked me about this matter that I could not imagine that they would bring such an opponent upon themselves without coercion while already fighting half of the

world. I told Colonel Röhricht the same thing some days later in Nancy.' *See also* Heinrici's diary entry, 10 November 1942, ibid: 'They should have made them allies, even at the cost of the straits, the Dardanelles, the Russian war has used too much German power and occupies too much of it.'

7. Curt Freiherr von Gienanth (1876–1961), General of the Cavalry. Military commander of the General Government from July 1940 to September 1942.
8. Hans Frank (1900–1946, executed), Governor General from October 1939 to January 1945.
9. The town Rawa Mazowiecka where Heinrici was positioned in 1914–1915. At that time Lieutenant Colonel von Selle was his superior.
10. On the ghetto in Siedlce *see* Kazimierski: 'Okupacja', pp. 160f. Before the war almost half of the city's population was Jewish, around 15,000 people. In 1940 the German occupier set up a forced labour camp and in 1941 a ghetto. Until April 1943 the Jews from Siedlce were murdered there or deported to the nearby Treblinka extermination camp.
11. Günther von Kluge (1882–1944), Field Marshal, from September 1939 to December 1941 commander-in-chief of the 4th Army, from December 1941 to October 1943 commander-in-chief of Army Group Centre.
12. Walther von Brauchitsch (1881–1948), Field Marshal, from February 1938 to December 1941 commander-in-chief of the army.
13. On 16 June 1941 all German consulates in the United States were ordered to be closed and their staff to leave the country by 10 July.
14. During the Finnish–Soviet Winter War from 30 November 1939 to 12 March 1940 the vastly superior Red Army was able to force a peace treaty on Finland only after huge and unexpected losses and enormous efforts. This failure led the Germans to underestimate the Red Army.
15. *See also* Halder: *War Journal*, vol. VI, p. 196 (3 July 1941): 'It is thus probably no overstatement to say that the Russian campaign has been won in the space of two weeks. Of course, this does not yet mean that it is closed. The sheer geographical vastness of the country and the stubbornness of the resistance, which is carried on with all means, will claim our efforts for

many more weeks to come (http://cgsc.contentdm.oclc.org/utils/getfile/collection/p4013coll8/id/3973/filename/3983.pdf).

16. The Fieseler Fi 56 Storch (stork) was a small and versatile cabin aeroplane for three people. A short take-off and landing aircraft, it was built as a surveillance and liaison aircraft for high-ranking staff officers ('flying *Kübelwagen*').
17. On the killing of German POWs, *see* Zayas: *Wehrmacht-Untersuchungsstelle*, pp. 273–307; *DRZW*, vol. 4, pp. 784–9.
18. On 3 July 1941 Stalin, in his well-known broadcast address to the nation, called on a 'patriotic war of defence' and ordered every item of value to be destroyed. This scorched earth strategy not only hindered the German advance, but also worsened the living conditions of the population in these areas. See *DRZW*, vol. 4, pp. 731–3.
19. Maximilian Freiherr von Weichs (1881–1954), Colonel-General, from October 1939 to July 1942 commander-in-chief of the 2nd Army.
20. Fedor von Bock (1880–1945), Field Marshal, from April to December 1941 commander-in-chief of Army Group Centre, from January to July 1942 commander-in-chief of Army Group South.
21. Lance Corporal Balzen, Heinrici's orderly.
22. Little is known about the military occupation policy in the area of Army Group Centre during these months. For reference *see* earlier accounts: Dallin: *Herrschaft*; Reitlinger: *Haus*; Müller: *Wehrmacht*. *See also* Schulte: *Army*; Pohl: *Herrschaft*. For Belarus *see* Gerlach: *Morde*.
23. Hartmut Heinrici (born 1921), an infantryman, was wounded on 15 July 1941 at the capture of Smolensk. After his recovery, at the end of November he was again deployed in the central area of the Eastern Front.
24. On the development of the partisan movement consisting predominantly of scattered Soviet soldiers, escaped POWs, members of the annihilation battalions, and civilians persecuted by Germans, *see* Hesse: *Partisanenkrieg*, pp. 38–70. *See also* Armstrong: *Partisans*; Grenkevich: *Partisan Movement*; Shepherd: *War*.
25. For July 1941 alone, the statistical study by Rüdiger Overmans puts the war dead of the German army at 63,099. The casualty figure for the first quarter of the campaign was 185,198,

i.e. 6.8 per cent of the Eastern Army, or 2,060 daily. *See* Overmans: *Verluste*, pp. 277–9.

26. *See also* Halder, *War Journal*, vol. VII, p. 36 (11 August 1941): 'The whole situation makes it increasingly plain that we have underestimated the Russian Colossus, who consistently prepared for war with that utterly ruthless determination so characteristic of totalitarian States' (http://cgsc.contentdm.oclc.org/utils/getfile/collection/p4013coll8/id/3974/filename/3984.pdf).
27. Literally: 'wet garden'. The workers' quarter in the industrial harbour in the southwest of Königsberg.
28. Lieutenant Beutelsbacher, interpreter in the Ic (intelligence, defence) department of the General Command.
29. Eugen Ritter von Schobert (1883–1941), Colonel-General, from October 1940 to September 1941 commander-in-chief of the 11th Army. On 12 September 1941 Schobert hit a mine while landing his *Fieseler Storch*.
30. Erich von Lewinski, called von Manstein (1887–1973), General of the Infantry, from March to September 1941 commanding general of the LVI Army Corps, from September 1941 to November 1942 commander-in-chief of the 11th Army.
31. An order by the OKH (*Oberkommando des Heeres*, Army High Command) signed by Quartermaster General Wagner had already prepared the dismissal of *Volksdeutscher* prisoners of war: Ukrainians, Lithuanians, Latvians, Estonians (IfZ, MA 1564, roll 31, NOKW-2423). In the following months it also applied to Belorussians among others and was implemented by the OKH first and foremost to secure the harvest.
32. On 18 September 1941 Heinrici was decorated with the Iron Cross. On 10 August 1941, at the head of his corps, he had led his men over the River Berezina and a day later they crossed the River Dnieper in rubber dinghies. Thus they arrived at the Gomel–Slobin railway line and enabled the encirclement of Gomel.
33. Friedrich Schulz (born in 1897), Colonel, from April 1940 to May 1942 chief of the General Staff of the XXXXIII Army Corps.
34. Walter von Reichenau (1884–1942), Field Marshal, from October 1939 to January 1942 commander-in-chief of the 6th Army, from December 1941 to January 1942 of Army Group South.

35. Semyon Konstantinovich Timoshenko (1895–1970), Marshal, from September 1941 to July 1942 commander-in-chief of the Soviet Southwestern Front.
36. After the German army had captured Kiev on 19 September 1941, several bombs prepared by the Red Army were detonated remotely which caused major fires and substantial casualties. The Germans reacted by taking harsh reprisals against 'partisans and Jews'. The mass murder at Babi Yar has probably to be seen in this context. *See DRZW*, vol. 4, pp. 514–16; Rüß: *Massaker*.
37. *See also* Hitler's appeal 'Soldiers of the Eastern Front!' on the 'start of the last decisive battle of this year' on 2 October 1941, in: BA-MA, RH 20-9/22. Again Hitler justified the campaign as a European pre-emptive war against 'Jewish Bolshevism', as 'a joint action to save the most precious culture continent'. The 'whole of Europe would have been lost. Because this enemy is not soldiers but mainly beasts.'
38. The capture of Odessa was not completed until 16 October 1941 after two months of siege by the 4th Romanian Army.
39. Heinz Guderian (1888–1954), Colonel-General, from November 1940 to October 1941 commander of Panzer Group 2, from October to December 1941 commander-in-chief of the 2nd Panzer Army.
40. The German campaign against Yugoslavia and Greece started on 6 April 1941. Yugoslavia capitulated as early as 17 April 1941, and by 30 April the Greek mainland was occupied. By 1 June British troops had left Crete. The attack against the Soviet Union, initially planned for late May 1941, was postponed for several weeks due to the Balkan campaign. Even now there is debate about the exact length of the delay, but it is fair to assume that it was not much longer than four weeks, as was taken into account by Halder. *See* Halder: *Kriegstagebuch*, vol. 2, p. 332 (28 March 1941).
41. *See also* Buchbender: *Erz*, passim.
42. After experiencing the detonations in Kiev, Hitler on 7 October 1941 gave orders that Moscow, Leningrad and other major cities were not to be occupied, but rather bypassed, encircled and destroyed by artillery shelling. *See DRZW*, vol. 4, pp. 515f.
43. Günther Blumentritt (1892–1967), Colonel, from October 1940 to January 1942 Chief of Staff of the 4th Army. Heinrici visited him in his headquarters in Yukhnov on that day.

44. On the prolonged disputes from mid-July to mid-August 1941 on whether the objective should be Moscow (Brauchitsch, Halder, Bock) or the southern industrial area (Hitler, OKW), which caused a degree of operative stagnation, *see DRZW*, vol. 4, pp. 489–96, pp. 503–7; Hartmann: *Halder*, pp. 278–84.
45. *See* Guderian: *Panzerleader*. 'General Heinrici, always a practical and sensible man, who commands the XXXXIII Army Corps, now came to see me [on 29 October] and described the bad conditions of his troops' supplies; among other things there had been no issue of bread since October 20th.'
46. Since July 1937 Japan had been fighting an undeclared war against China and occupied vast territories of the huge country without being able to defeat it entirely.
47. *See also* Hesse: *Partisanenkrieg*, pp. 53f.
48. A village between Kaluga and Tula, about 50km northwest of Tula.
49. Johannes Graf Moy (1902–1995), writer, from 1941 to 1942 *Sonderführer* (Specialist Leader) and interpreter of the General Command of the XXXXIII Army Corps.
50. As early as the beginning of October Heinrici had tried to get winter clothing for his corps. *See also* his diary entry for 10 October 1941. *See also* Guderian: *Panzerleader*: 'On 16 November General Heinrici visited me: frost damages, shortage of clothing, being lice-ridden.'
51. *See also* Heinrici's war report to his family, 11 December 1941.
52. Ewald von Kleist (1881–1954), Colonel-General, from October 1941 to September 1942 commander-in-chief of the 1st Panzer Army.
53. Otto Drescher (1885–1944), Lieutenant-Colonel, from October 1940 commander of Infantry-Regiment 434 (131st Infantry Division).
54. The Soviet 'Katyusha' rocket launcher (known as *Stalinorgel;* Stalin organs).
55. The road between Tula and Moscow.
56. Friedrich Hoßbach (1894–1980), Colonel, former Hitler's military adjutant, from October 1939 to January 1942 commander of Infantry Regiment 82. On the attack of his regiment on 5 December 1941, which involved heavy losses, *see* Hoßbach: *Infanterie*, pp. 156–66.

57. In late November Guderian repeatedly demanded at least one additional division for the attack on Tula. *See DRZW*, vol. 4, p. 597.
58. On 18 December 1941 Hitler forbade any withdrawal in his so-called 'Haltebefehl'.
59. The attack on Moscow had come to a standstill everywhere on 5 December; the Red Army's counteroffensive started the same day. On 8 December Hitler ordered the offensive to cease and the troops to go onto the defensive (Fuehrer's directive no. 39). On the Soviet counteroffensive and the German winter crisis until the stabilization of the front in the first half of February 1942, *see* Reinhardt: *Wende*, pp. 197–254; *DRZW*, vol. 4, pp. 600–52.
60. As early as 28 November the 1st Panzer Army (Kleist) had to leave Rostov. *See* Reinhardt: *Wende*, pp. 177f.
61. On 7 December 1941 Japan had started the war against the USA with a surprise air raid on the American naval base at Pearl Harbor on the Hawaii island of Oahu.
62. Erwin Rommel (1891–1944), General of the Panzer Army, from February 1941 commanding general of the Afrika Korps.
63. *See also* Guderian: *Panzerleader*. In early December Guderian established his advance command post on this estate, Yasnaya Polyana, for a couple of days.
64. The *Reichskommissariate* (realm commissariats) Ostland and Ukraine.
65. After Japan's attack on Pearl Harbor (7 December) and the USA's subsequent declaration of war on Japan (8 December), Germany and Italy declared war on the USA on 11 December.
66. On 16 December 1941 Hitler informed Army Group Centre that he had effectively taken over the High Command of the Army himself. Officially it was not until 19 December that the High Command devolved from Brauchitsch to Hitler. *See* Reinhardt: *Wende*, p. 223.
67. Wilhelm Keitel (1882–1946), Field Marshal, from February 1938 to May 1945 Supreme Commander of the Armed Forces (*Oberkommando der Wehrmacht, OKW*). Keitel was executed in 1946.
68. Hans Felber (1889–1962), General of the Infantry, from October 1940 to January 1942 commanding general of the XIII Army Corps. He was Heinrici's neighbour on the left.

69. *See* Hitler's order on 18 December 1941, in: *KTB/OKW*, vol. 1, pp. 1084f. 'Major withdrawal movements are not to be conducted. They will result in the complete loss of heavy weapons and equipment. Under the personal leadership of commanders and officers alike, the troops are to be forced to put up a fanatical resistance in their lines, regardless of any enemy breakthrough in their flanks and rear.'
70. From December 1941 to January 1942 commander-in-chief of the 4th Army. On 26 December 1941 Kübler superseded Kluge, who had succeeded Bock as commander-in-chief of Army Group Centre on 18 December.
71. Headquarters of the 4th Army.
72. After reporting to Hitler, Kübler was replaced by Heinrici on 20 January 1942 because he considered it impossible to hold the 'winter position' without further withdrawal movements and did not feel up to the situation. *See* Reinhardt: *Wende*, p. 251.
73. In December 1941 Rommel conducted an orderly withdrawal to the west with his Afrika Korps and his Italian allies to evade the British offensive. As early as 22 January 1942 he successfully counterattacked.
74. Walter von Unruh (1877–1956), Lieutenant-General, from September 1941 to May 1942 commander of the Rear Area Army Territory 559 of the 2nd Army.
75. Refers to a poem by Gustav Schwab, *Der Reiter und der Bodensee*, about a rider who rides across the frozen Lake Constance unaware that he is no longer on land. It hints at a daring enterprise unknowingly undertaken.
76. From 24 June 1941 the Fuehrer's *Wolfsschanze* headquarters lay in Rastenburg/East Prussia. Heinrici and the other commanders in chief of the centre section of the Eastern Front were asked to report there. *See* Halder: *Kriegstagebuch*, vol. 3, p. 407 (28 February 1942).
77. Franz Halder (1884–1972), Colonel-General, from September 1938 to September 1942 chief of the OKH General Staff.
78. There is a similar discussion about the differences between the mood on the front and in the homeland in Stieff's letter (General Staff officer of the 4th Army) to his wife, 7 December 1941, in: Stieff, *Briefe*, pp. 138–41.
79. In January 1942 an army of 20,000 men, comprising parts of the First Guard Cavalry Corps, airborne troops and partisans,

emerged in the rear of the 4th Army within the triangle Smolensk–Vyazma–Spas Demensk. These troops, commanded by General Below, could not be annihilated before June 1942 (Operation Hanover). *See DRZW*, vol. 6, pp. 865f.

80. Heinz von Gyldenfeldt (1899–1971), Colonel, from June 1941 to May 1942 1st General Staff officer OKH. From his time as chief of operations (Ia) in the General Staff of the 16th Division in Münster (1938/39), Gyldenfeldt was acquainted with Heinrici and his wife.
81. Gisela Heinrici (born 1926), Heinrici's daughter.
82. Gerhard Berthold (1891–1942), Major General, from August 1941 to 14 April 1942 commander of the 31st Infantry Division.
83. Major General Blumentritt, chief of staff of the 4th Army, was appointed Chief Quartermaster I of the General Staff OKH on 18 January 1942.
84. *See* Heinrici's diary entry, 28 April 1942, in: BA-MA, N 265/13: 'Attack on Pawlowo by the 98th Division failed. I left the last preparation meeting yesterday thinking: everything humanly possible has been done. And yet: failure. ... Depression everywhere. I have to say that I am shaken. Twelve officers and 458 men out of 850 lost, and all in vain.'
85. On 10 June 1942 Heinrici temporarily handed over his command to Infantry General Hans von Salmuth and took extended leave in Germany. On 20 July 1942 he returned to his post.

Archival Sources

Bundesarchiv-Militärarchiv, Freiburg/Br. (BA-MA)
Nachlass Hans Felber (N 67)
N 67/1: Tagebücher, 1939–1945.
Nachlass Gotthard Heinrici (N 265)
N 265/8: Tagebücher, vol. 1, 1896–1906, 1917–1919.
N 265/9: ibid, vol. 2, 1938–1940.
N 265/10: ibid, vol. 3, June 1940–April 1941.
N 265/11: ibid, vol. 4, July–December 1941.
N 265/12: ibid, vol. 5, Maschinenabschriften, September–December 1941.
N 265/13: ibid, vol. 6, January 1942–July 1943.
N 265/14: ibid, vol. 7, January–July 1942.
N 265/15: ibid, vol. 8, January–June 1944.
N 265/16: Maschinenabschriften aus Tagebüchern und Briefen, April–September 1941.
N 265/23: Aufzeichnungen, vol. 2: Erster Weltkrieg, 1941, 1959–1962.
N 265/24: ibid, vol. 3: Erinnerungen eines alten Gumbinners, 1960.
N 265/26: ibid, vol. 5: Militärische Laufbahn und Zweiter Weltkrieg, 1966.
N 265/31: ibid.: Erlebnisse in Königsberg 1919–1922, 1961.
N 265/33: Ansprachen, 1930–1939.
N 265/35: Schriftwechsel, 1932–1944.
N 265/43: Notizen, August–December 1943.
N 265/46: Vorgänge um den Rückzug aus Smolensk, 1944.
N 265/57: Ermittlungsverfahren gegen den Führer des Sk 7b Rabe, 1968.
N 265/114: Niederschriften, 1947.
N 265/147: Briefe an die Eltern, vol. 4, 1930–1932.
N 265/148: ibid, vol. 5, 1933.
N 265/149: ibid, vol. 6, 1934.
N 265/151: ibid, vol. 8, 1937.
N 265/152: Briefe an Mutter und Schwiegermutter, vol. 1, 1938.

N 265/153: ibid, vol. 2, 1939.
N 265/154: Briefe an Gattin und Kinder, vol. 1, 1924–1940.
N 265/155: ibid, vol. 2, 1941.
N 265/156: ibid, vol. 3, 1942.
N 265/157: ibid, vol. 4, 1943.
N 265/158: ibid, vol. 5, 1944–1946.

Personalakten (Pers)

Pers 6/30: Gotthard Heinrici.

Akten der Heeresdienststellen (RH)

RH 20–9/22: 9. Armee, Anlagen zum KTB Nr. 3, vol. 4, June–December 1941.
RH 24–43: XXXXIII. Armeekorps.

Institut für Zeitgeschichte, München (IfZ)

MA 1564: Nürnberger Dokumente, Rolle 29, 31.
MA 1569: Nürnberg Interrogations, Rolle 26.
ZS 66/2: Zeugenschrifttum Gotthard Heinrici.

Bibliography

Armstrong, John (ed.): *Soviet Partisans in World War II* (Madison, Wisc.: 1964).

Bitzel, Uwe: *Die Konzeption des Blitzkrieges bei der deutschen Wehrmacht* (Frankfurt/M. [et. al.]: 1991).

Brausch, Günter & Hubatsch, Walter: 'Gotthard Heinrici', in: *Altpreußische Biographie*, vol. 3 (Marburg/Lahn: 1975) pp. 949f.

Buchbender, Ortwin: *Das tönende Erz. Deutsche Propaganda gegen die Rote Armee im Zweiten Weltkrieg* (Stuttgart: 1978).

Dallin, Alexander: *Deutsche Herrschaft in Rußland 1941–1945. Eine Studie über Besatzungspolitik* (Düsseldorf: 1958).

DRZW: Das Deutsche Reich und der Zweite Weltkrieg, ed. for Militärgeschichtliches Forschungsamt.

vol. 4: Horst Boog [et al.]: *Der Angriff auf die Sowjetunion* (Stuttgart: 1983).

vol. 5/1: Bernhard R. Kroener [et al.]: *Organisation und Mobilisierung des deutschen Machtbereichs. Kriegsverwaltung, Wirtschaft und personelle Ressourcen 1939–1941* (Stuttgart: 1988).

vol. 6: Horst Boog [et al.]: *Der Globale Krieg. Die Ausweitung zum Weltkrieg und der Wechsel der Initiative 1941–1943* (Stuttgart: 1990).

'Fahrtberichte' aus der Zeit des deutsch-sowjetischen Krieges 1941, Protokolle des Begleitoffiziers des Kommandierenden Generals LIII. Armeekorps, introd. and ed. Walther Lammers (Boppard/Rhine: 1988).

Fall Barbarossa. Dokumente zur Vorbereitung der faschistischen Wehrmacht auf die Aggression gegen die Sowjetunion (1940/41), introd. Erhard Moritz (Berlin [Ost]: 1970).

Förster, Gerhard: *Totaler Krieg und Blitzkrieg. Die Theorie des totalen Krieges und des Blitzkrieges in der Militärdoktrin des faschistischen Deutschlands am Vorabend des Zweiten Weltkrieges* (Berlin [Ost]: 1967).

Förster, Jürgen: 'Zum Rußlandbild der Militärs 1941–1945', in: *Das Rußlandbild im Dritten Reich*, ed. Hans-Erich Volkmann (Cologne/Weimar/Vienna: 1994), pp. 141–63.

Friedrich, Jörg: *Das Gesetz des Krieges. Das deutsche Heer in Rußland 1941–1945. Der Prozeß gegen das Oberkommando der Wehrmacht* (Munich: 1993).

Frieser, Karl-Heinz: *Blitzkrieg-Legende. Der Westfeldzug 1940* (Munich: 1996).

Fritz, Stephen G.: *Ostkrieg. Hitler's War of Extermination in the East* (Lexington, KY: 2011).

Generalfeldmarschall Fedor von Bock. Zwischen Pflicht und Verweigerung. Das Kriegstagebuch, ed. Klaus Gerbet (Munich/Berlin: 1995).

Generalfeldmarschall Wilhelm Ritter von Leeb. Tagebuchaufzeichnungen und Lagebeurteilungen aus zwei Weltkriegen, ed. and provided with biographical notes by Georg Meyer (Stuttgart: 1976).

Gerlach, Christian: *Kalkulierte Morde. Die deutsche Wirtschafts- und Vernichtungspolitik in Weißrußland 1941 bis 1944* (Hamburg: 1999).

Geyer, Michael: *Aufrüstung oder Sicherheit. Die Reichswehr in der Krise der Machtpolitik 1924–1936* (Wiesbaden: 1980).

Glantz, David M.: *Operation Barbarossa. Hitler's Invasion of Russia 1941* (Brimscombe Port: 2011).

Grenkevich, Leonid: *The Soviet Partisan Movement 1941–1944. A Critical Historiographical Analysis* (London/Portland, Or.: 1999).

Guderian, Heinz: *Erinnerungen eines Soldaten* (Heidelberg: 1951).

Guderian, Heinz: *Panzerleader. The classic account of Blitzkrieg* (London: 2009).

Halder, Generaloberst: *Kriegstagebuch. Tägliche Aufzeichnungen des Chefs des Generalstabes des Heeres 1939–1942*, ed. Arbeitskreis für Wehrforschung and Hans-Adolf Jacobsen [Engl. translation: Franz Halder: *War Journal of Franz Halder*, 8 vols (United States: A.G. EUCOM, 1947) http://cgsc.contentdm.oclc.org/utils/getfile/collection/p4013coll8/id/3973/filename/3983.pdf]:

- vol. 1: *Vom Polenfeldzug bis zum Ende der Westoffensive (14 August 1939–30 June 1940)* (Stuttgart: 1962).
- vol. 2: *Von der geplanten Landung in England bis zum Beginn des Ostfeldzuges (1 July 1940–21 June 1941)* (Stuttgart: 1963).
- vol. 3: *Der Rußlandfeldzug bis zum Marsch auf Stalingrad (22 June 1941–24 September 1942)* (Stuttgart: 1964).

Hartmann, Christian: *Halder. Generalstabschef Hitlers 1938–1942* (Paderborn [et al.]: 1991).

Hartmann, Christian: *Wehrmacht im Ostkrieg. Front und militärisches Hinterland 1941/42* (2nd edn; Munich: 2010).

Hartmann, Christian: *Operation Barbarossa: Nazi Germany's War in the East 1941–1945* (Oxford: 2013).

Heeresdruckvorschrift (H.Dv.g 92): Handbuch für den Generalstabsdienst im Kriege, part 1 (Berlin: 1939).

Heeresdruckvorschrift (H.Dv. 300/1): Truppenführung, part 1 (Berlin: 1936).

Hesse, Erich: *Der sowjetrussische Partisanenkrieg 1941 bis 1944 im Spiegel deutscher Kampfanweisungen und Befehle* (Göttingen: 1969).

Hillgruber, Andreas: *Hitler, König Carol und Marschall Antonescu. Die deutsch-rumänischen Beziehungen 1938–1944* (Wiesbaden: 1954).

Hoßbach, Friedrich: *Infanterie im Ostfeldzug 1941/42* (Osterode/Harz: 1951).

Hürter, Johannes: *Hitlers Heerführer. Die deutschen Oberbefehlshaber im Krieg gegen die Sowjetunion 1941/42* (2nd edn; Munich: 2007).

Kazimierski, Józef: 'Okupacja i zbrodnie hitlerowskie na Podlasiu w latach 1939–1944', in: *Okreg Siedlecki 1942–1944* (Warsaw: 1977), pp. 148–79.

Kroener, Bernhard R.: 'Strukturelle Veränderungen in der militärischen Gesellschaft des Dritten Reiches', in: *Nationalsozialismus und Modernisierung*, ed. Michael Prinz & Rainer Zitelmann (Darmstadt 2nd edn; 1994), pp. 267–96.

KTB/OKW: *Kriegstagebuch des Oberkommandos der Wehrmacht (Wehrmachtsführungsstab)*, vol. 1: *1 August 1940–31 December 1941*, ed. Hans-Adolf Jacobsen (Frankfurt/M.: 1965).

Merridale, Catherine: *Ivan's War. The Red Army, 1941–45* (London: 2005).

Messerschmidt, Manfred: *Die Wehrmacht im NS-Staat. Zeit der Indoktrination* (Hamburg: 1969).

Möller-Witten, Hans: 'Gotthard Heinrici', in idem: *Mit dem Eichenlaub zum Ritterkreuz. Aus dem Leben von zwanzig vorbildlichen Soldaten* (Rastatt: 1962), pp. 165–74.

Müller, Klaus-Jürgen: *Das Heer und Hitler. Armee und nationalsozialistisches Regime 1933–1940* (Stuttgart: 1969).

Müller, Klaus-Jürgen: 'Armee und Drittes Reich. Versuch einer historischen Interpretation', in idem: *Armee, Politik und Gesellschaft in Deutschland 1933–1945. Studien zum Verhältnis von Armee und NS-System* (Paderborn: 1979), pp. 11–50.

Müller, Klaus-Jürgen: *Armee und Drittes Reich 1933–1939. Darstellung und Dokumentation* (Paderborn: 1987).

Müller, Norbert: *Wehrmacht und Okkupation 1941–1944. Zur Rolle der Wehrmacht und ihrer Führungsorgane im Okkupationsregime des faschistischen deutschen Imperialismus auf sowjetischem Territorium* (Berlin [Ost]: 1971).

Müller-Hillebrandt, Burkhart: *Das Heer 1933–1945. Entwicklung des organisatorischen Aufbaues*, vol. 1: *Das Heer bis zum Kriegsbeginn* (Darmstadt: 1954).

Overmans, Rüdiger: *Deutsche militärische Verluste im Zweiten Weltkrieg* (Munich: 1999).

Petter, Wolfgang: 'Militärische Massengesellschaft und Entprofessionalisierung des Offiziers', in: *Die Wehrmacht. Mythos und Realität*, ed. for Militärgeschichtliches Forschungsamts by Rolf-Dieter Müller and Hans-Erich Volkmann (Munich: 1999), pp. 359–70.

Philippi, Alfred: 'Generaloberst Heinrici – 80 Jahre alt', in *Wehrwissenschaftliche Rundschau 16* (1966), pp. 661–5.

Pohl, Dieter: *Die Herrschaft der Wehrmacht. Deutsche Militärbesatzung und einheimische Bevölkerung in der Sowjetunion 1941–1944* (Munich: 2008).

Reinhardt, Klaus: *Die Wende vor Moskau. Das Scheitern der Strategie Hitlers im Winter 1941/42* (Stuttgart: 1972).

Reitlinger, Gerald: *Ein Haus auf Sand gebaut. Hitlers Gewaltpolitik in Rußland 1941–1944* (Hamburg: 1962).

Römer, Felix: *Der Kommissarbefehl. Wehrmacht und NS-Verbrechen an der Ostfront 1941/42* (Paderborn: 2008).

Rüß, Hartmut: 'Wer war verantwortlich für das Massaker von Babij Jar?' in: *Militärgeschichtliche Mitteilungen* 57 (1998), no. 2, pp. 483–508.

Ryan, Cornelius: *Der letzte Kampf* (Munich/Zurich: 1966).

Schulte, Theo J.: *The German Army and Nazi Policies in Occupied Russia* (Oxford [et al.]: 1989).

Shepherd, Ben: *War in the Wild East. The German Army and Soviet Partisans* (Cambridge, MA: 2004).

Speer, Albert: *Erinnerungen* (Frankfurt/M/Berlin: 1969).

Stahel, David: *Operation Barbarossa and Germany's Defeat in the East* (Cambridge: 2009).

Stahel, David: *Kiev 1941. Hitler's Battle for Supremacy in the East* (Cambridge: 2012).

Stahel, David: *Operation Typhoon. Hitler's March on Moscow* (Cambridge: 2013).

Stieff, Hellmuth: *Briefe*, ed. and introd. Horst Mühleisen (Berlin: 1991).
Streim, Alfred: *Die Behandlung sowjetischer Kriegsgefangener im 'Fall Barbarossa'. Eine Dokumentation* (Heidelberg/Karlsruhe: 1981).
Streit, Christian: *Keine Kameraden. Die Wehrmacht und die sowjetischen Kriegsgefangenen 1941–1945* (Stuttgart: 1978).
Taysen, Adalbert v.: 'Krieg', in: *Handbuch der neuzeitlichen Wehrwissenschaften*, ed. for *Deutsche Gesellschaft für Wehrpolitik und Wehrwissenschaften* by Hermann Franke, vol. 1, (Berlin/Leipzig: 1936), pp. 171–5.
Thomas, Franz: *Die Eichenlaub-Träger 1940–1945*, vol. 1 (Osnabrück: 1997).
Wegner, Bernd: 'Defensive ohne Strategie. Die Wehrmacht und das Jahr 1943', in: *Die Wehrmacht. Mythos und Realität*, ed. for Militärgeschichtliches Forschungsamts by Rolf-Dieter Müller and Hans-Erich Volkmann (Munich: 1999), pp. 197–209.
de Zayas, Alfred M.: *Die Wehrmacht-Untersuchungsstelle. Deutsche Ermittlungen über alliierte Völkerrechtsverletzungen im Zweiten Weltkrieg*, in cooperation with Walter Rabus (Munich 3rd edn: 1980).